THE LITTLE BOOK

OF
IMPACT INVESTING

Little Book Big Profits Series

In the Little Book series, the brightest icons in the financial world write on topics that range from tried-and-true investment strategies to tomorrow's new trends. Each book offers a unique perspective on investing, allowing the reader to pick and choose from the very best in investment advice today.

Books in the Little Book series include:

The Little Book of Investing Like the Pros by Pearl and Rosenbaum
The Little Book That Still Beats the Market by Joel Greenblatt
The Little Book That Saves Your Assets by David M. Darst
The Little Book That Builds Wealth by Pat Dorsey
The Little Book That Makes You Rich by Louis Navellier
The Little Book of Common Sense Investing by John C. Bogle
The Little Book of Value Investing by Christopher Browne
The Little Book of Big Dividends by Charles B. Carlson
The Little Book of Main Street Money by Jonathan Clements
The Little Book of Trading by Michael W. Covel
The Little Book of Valuation by Aswath Damodaran
The Little Book of Economics by Greg Ip
The Little Book of Sideways Markets by Vitaliy N. Katsenelson
The Little Book of Big Profits from Small Stocks by Hilary Kramer
The Little Book of Currency Trading by Kathy Lien
The Little Book of Bull's Eye Investing by John Mauldin
The Little Book of Emerging Markets by Mark Mobius
The Little Book of Behavioral Investing by James Montier
The Little Book of Hedge Funds by Anthony Scaramucci
The Little Book of Bull Moves by Peter D. Schiff
The Little Book of Alternative Investments by Stein and DeMuth
The Little Book of Bulletproof Investing by Ben Stein and Phil DeMuth
The Little Book of Commodity Investing by John R. Stephenson
The Little Book of the Shrinking Dollar by Addison Wiggin
The Little Book of Stock Market Profits by Mitch Zacks
The Little Book of Safe Money by Jason Zweig
The Little Book of Zen Money by The Seven Dollar Millionaire
The Little Book of Picking Top Stocks by Martin S. Fridson
The Little Book of Robo Investing by Elizabeth MacBride and Quian Liu
The Little Book of Trading Options Like the Pros by David Berns and Michael Green

THE LITTLE BOOK

OF

IMPACT INVESTING

*Aligning Profit and Purpose to
Change the World*

Priya Parrish

WILEY

Published by John Wiley & Sons, Inc., Hoboken, New Jersey.
Published simultaneously in Canada.

For general information on our other products and services or for technical support, please contact our Customer Care Department within the United States at (800) 762-2974, outside the United States at (317) 572-3993 or fax (317) 572-4002.

Wiley also publishes its books in a variety of electronic formats. Some content that appears in print may not be available in electronic formats. For more information about Wiley products, visit our web site at www.wiley.com.

Library of Congress Cataloging-in-Publication Data is Available

ISBN 9781394257560 (Cloth)
ISBN 9781394257584 (ePDF)
ISBN 9781394257577 (ePub)

COVER DESIGN: PAUL MCCARTHY

SKY10082223_082024

To Mom and Dad, for inspiring a higher purpose.
To Rebecca, for helping me find my path.
To Sai, Aadi, and Diya, for making sure I'm still having fun.

Table of Contents

Preface   xi

PART ONE
**A BRIEF INTRODUCTION
  TO IMPACT INVESTING**   1

Chapter One
What Is Impact Investing?   3

Chapter Two
**Why Now? The Right Time for
  Creative Disruption**   19

Chapter Three
Hold On, What About ESG?   31

Chapter Four
My Journey to Impact Investing   43

Chapter Five
How Impact Investing Grew Up   53

Chapter Six
Who Can Be an Impact Investor?   67

Chapter Seven
Other Roads to the Same Place   79

PART TWO
**HOW TO BE AN IMPACT
   INVESTOR**   89

Chapter Eight
How Impact Can Drive Returns   91

Chapter Nine
**Where Do You Start? Deciding Where
   Impact Belongs in Your Portfolio**   101

Chapter Ten
**Beyond the Label: Identifying
    Impactful Companies**   109

Chapter Eleven
If You Don't Measure It, Is It Real?   119

Chapter Twelve
**Building Better Businesses: Impact
    Management**   131

Chapter Thirteen
**Stuck in the Mud: When Impact
    Gets Complicated**   143

PART THREE
**THE IMPACT OPPORTUNITY
    SET**   153

Chapter Fourteen
**Where Can You Find Impact
    Investments?**   155

Chapter Fifteen
Economic Opportunity   161

Chapter Sixteen
Health and Wellness   175

Chapter Seventeen
Environmental Sustainability   189

Chapter Eighteen
Public Markets   201

Chapter Nineteen
Social Impact Bonds   211

Chapter Twenty
Alternative Ownership Structures   217

Conclusion   229

Notes   235

Acknowledgments   249

About the Author   253

Preface

———— ≈ ————

Wiley's Little Book series has a long history of sharing finance strategies in understandable terms. The addition of impact investing to the series is an important milestone as it cements this once controversial idea as a widely accepted, powerful, and more thoughtful way to invest.

Impact investing, a term coined in 2007, allows investors to do social and environmental good while still making a profit.[1] What was once seen as a radical idea is now common sense. Businesses that solve society's biggest challenges are financially valuable and often make for great investment opportunities. As impact investing gains more adherents and credibility, it is time for it to be well understood and utilized by everyone.

This book is my attempt to make sense of the confusion, as it is difficult for a newcomer to understand the jargon, sort through the many false or exaggerated claims, and follow the heated debates about this topic. It is written for anyone who expects more than financial returns from their investments or is curious about what their investments can do when aligned with purpose.

There are many reasons why you might want to become an impact investor. First, it has the potential to enhance your returns and lower your risk. Impact investing, like entrepreneurship, centers around disrupting the status quo with more effective solutions. Moreover, taking this approach can help you avoid investing in companies that are taking unnecessary risks (e.g. in the way they misman-age their employee base and culture or are exposed to costly environmental hazards in their supply chain).

Impact investments are also a more efficient way to achieve social goals. It's inefficient to disregard the social impact of how you invest and expect philanthropy or gov-ernment programs to deal with any negative effects. Impact investing is a more effective use of capital because it consid-ers the long-term costs and benefits for investors and other stakeholders from the outset.

Finally, it's emotionally rewarding to align your values with your dollars. As Mahatma Gandhi said, "Happiness is when what you think, what you say, and what you do are in harmony." We seek this alignment in how we vote, what we buy, where we donate, and possibly even our choice of work. How we invest is another opportunity to live a life of integrity.

Regardless of your motivation, this book is intended to help define smart impact investing and give you a toolkit to become an effective impact investor. This might mean investing for yourself, pushing your financial advisor to do better for you, or inspiring the foundation board you sit on to align its finances with its mission. Impact investing is for everyone, regardless of values, political views, or how much they have to invest. If you do it well, it can make you a better investor, and I'm going to help you understand how.

My journey to impact investing began when I was an undergraduate student studying economics and entrepreneurship. I could not understand why we were so obviously underutilizing the power of business to improve the world. This was 20 years ago, before impact investing was a recognized strategy. At the time, just about everyone in the field was an entrepreneur experimenting with investment tools to do well financially and to do good for the world. I joined right in.

I'll share more about my journey in Chapter 4, but for now, you can rest assured knowing that I've been at this for many years and have done everything from investing in to managing and creating impact funds. Along the way, I have also spent years in the hedge fund and family office world, as I felt strongly that to be a good *impact* investor, you must be a *great* investor. Today, I serve as chief investment officer at Impact Engine, a $250 million institutional venture capital and private equity firm based in Chicago driving positive impact in economic opportunity, environmental sustainability, and health equity.

I've taught a course on impact investing for MBA students at the University of Chicago Booth School of Business for several years. Much of the content in this book comes from that curriculum. As the demand for that course grew, I added courses for executive MBA students, as well as for the accomplished leaders in the Leadership & Society Initiative who were transitioning their longstanding careers toward purposeful next chapters. The increasing demand for my courses underscores that society finally welcomes, and perhaps even expects, the business and finance community to be part of the solution to society's greatest challenges.

With more than $1 trillion of assets under management, according to the Global Impact Investing Network, the field is growing quickly, and many asset management firms are crowding into the space.[2] This includes pure-play funds completely dedicated to impact investing, as well as some of the largest diversified asset managers. From Bain Capital to Blackrock, investment firms have entered this field as it has become more proven and have catapulted it to one of the most in-demand investment strategies today. This means that today young professionals can go straight into impact investing, and so too can experienced professionals who want to apply their investment skills in a more mission-driven way.

While the industry tailwinds are strong, we are in an important period where the diverse approaches to impact investing need codification. Asset owners, from retail investors to pensions, drive demand, and asset managers respond with products, some better quality than others. This book will lay out not only what impact investing is, and how and why it has evolved to its current state, but also its limitations. I've intentionally included many examples of companies and funds striving to generate impact, both success stories and those that faced difficulties. It is important to note that I primarily discuss impact investing by venture capital and private equity investors in for-profit companies to simplify and focus the discussion. However, there is a long and successful history of philanthropic capital making other types of impact investments (including loans and guarantees) to bring economic opportunity to people and places not served by the financial sector.

Impact investing will inspire you, but it is not *the* solution to our society's challenges. We still require the government and philanthropy. We still need voters and volunteers. The rise of impact investing is about systems change, or how we can harness the massive power of the financial industry toward solving our most pressing problems. Impact investing is not easy; it is not perfect, but it is an underutilized and powerful tool that the world needs more of right now.

Part One

A Brief Introduction to Impact Investing

Chapter One

What Is Impact Investing?

LATELY, IT SEEMS LIKE every financial institution, from Vanguard to KKR, wants to sell you something with impact in the name. But with no clear definition of impact investing, how do you know if there is anything different about these investment funds? This also begs the question—what impact is each of these funds striving for? And do you agree with the goal?

There are also many mistruths and misconceptions about impact investing that lead to unsubstantiated skepticism.

One myth is that impact investing is a socialist conspiracy theory to redistribute wealth. Some critics conversely suggest impact investing is the capitalist way of extracting more profit from those in need. I've had people tell me it's only for liberals, and others say it's only for religious conservatives. It won't make money. It won't do good.

As impact investing found its way to mainstream media, I found it difficult to understand the logic behind such sensational and contradictory depictions. It's misunderstood, as the field has a long, winding history and a large tent that includes many approaches. I stumbled upon the idea 20 years ago and have had my own journey trying to figure out how to turn impact investing into a career. I can assure you, it does not have to be complicated, and you can apply it to your own portfolio if you break down the core principles.

Before I provide an accurate definition of impact investing, let me first set the record straight on some of the myths.

- **Myth: Impact investing won't make money, as you have to sacrifice returns to do something good.**

    Truth: It is possible to generate a range of financial returns while driving a positive impact. Many impact investments target returns that are in line with nonimpact investments. Other impact investments purposely target lower returns to create a type or amount of impact that otherwise wouldn't be possible but are often necessary to prove a market or catalyze future investment by those seeking market-rate returns. The common thread is an objective to create *some* amount of financial returns *and* social impact, with the investor needing to be clear about what amount of each in order to be held accountable for that.

- **Myth: Impact investing is just a marketing scheme.**

  Truth: Unfortunately, there are investment funds that use the label *impact investing* opportunistically with little to no intentional strategy or process to create any impact. However, those are simply bad investments. They don't define what one should expect. This same misbehavior can be found in other investment strategies and industries. I'm confident that with time those misusing the label will face consequences, from lawsuits to obsolescence.

- **Myth: Impact investing is a driver of woke capitalism.**

  Truth: The myth to bust here is the very idea of "woke capitalism," which is the belief that corporations seeking to communicate and operate in a way that is aligned with social goals—such as gender diversity, climate mitigation, or voting rights—is an overextension of their role in politics. Corporations have always tried to influence public policy. Just take a look at the billions of dollars spent yearly on lobbyists.[1] The rise of impact investing has also led to more CEOs feeling empowered and incentivized to speak up and change their management practices around impactful issues, making their involvement and position on topics more transparent to their employees, customers, and the public.

- **Myth: Impact investors are trying to displace philanthropy and nonprofits.**

    Truth: Nonprofits take on many challenges affecting vulnerable communities that only they can address, and philanthropy is an essential resource for this work. Impact investors believe that for-profit companies can help address or lessen many of the large challenges facing society and be partners to both philanthropy and government. Impact investing is not *the* solution, but it is an important part of the solution. For example, no amount of impact investing dollars will solve climate change; the challenges facing the planet require grant funding and other forms of philanthropic capital. Impact investors seek to provide an additional type of capital and alternative solutions to help mitigate and adapt to climate change.

- **Myth: You can't "prove" the impact of impact investing as it's not measurable.**

    Truth: Reputable impact investors can and do measure impact in accurate and verifiable ways. However, there are practical considerations, from cost to time horizon and privacy, that affect the level and type of measurement methodology. This variety in approach creates a lack of standardization, leading to the myth that measurement isn't possible. Foundations that provide philanthropic capital to nonprofits face the same measurement constraints despite decades of standardization attempts. Leaders in both impact investing and philanthropy support improvement in this area.

- **Myth: Impact investing is a fad, and real investors and business leaders don't care.**

   Truth: The consistent growth in impact assets under management throughout boom and bust markets shows no sign of waning (Figure 1.1). This trend is apparent in nearly every asset class and geography. The number of investment firms and business executives showing an interest in developing expertise or offering in this space supports that the industry is here to stay.

- **Myth: Impact investing is only for liberals, for the religious, for the rich, for the young, etc.**

   Truth: Impact investing is not a monolithic application but is based on a set of core principles to allow for a diversity of objectives and approaches.

   I don't know how this myth got started, as individuals and organizations of various social, religious, and economic statuses participate equally. For example, the Catholic Church and the Ford Foundation are known to invest their dollars in alignment with their unique missions. At Impact Engine, we have investors ranging from those in their 80s to those in their 20s, and often, generations come together within families to invest with impact.

- **Myth: Impact investing is a small market with limited options.**

   Truth: With more than $1 trillion of assets under management and growing, there is an increasing depth and breadth of impact investment options. As more dollars and talent roll into the field, this will only improve further. Many families and foundations, like the Nathan Cummings Foundation's $500 million endowment or the California Endowment's $4 billion, have already committed to investing all their capital with an impact lens.

Figure 1.1   Sizing the market

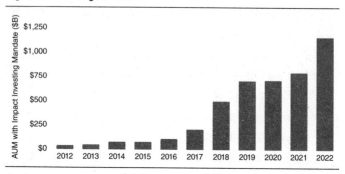

Source: GIIN Annual Impact Investor Survey. The GIIN. (2015–2022). https:// thegiin.org.

With some of the myth-busting now behind us, let's explore what defines an impact investment. While impact investing has a history rooted in the environmental, social, and governance (ESG) industry, which we will cover in Chapter 3, impact investing as a defined investment approach began in 2007 thanks to the leadership of the Rockefeller Foundation.

That year, the Rockefeller Foundation hired Anthony Bugg-Levine to lead a new effort in-house and brought together roughly 40 practitioners to their retreat center in Bellagio, Italy, to collaborate on bringing a clear definition to the marketplace.[2] They knew it was possible to drive impact outcomes with their investments, but there were such wide-ranging strategies and results that a unified view of impact investing was needed to understand its growing role in the portfolio.

For example, the Acumen Fund was started by Jacqueline Novogratz, who invested philanthropic dollars in revenue-generating social enterprises in East Africa and South Asia to recover most but not all of the capital invested.[3] Muhammad Yunus established the Grameen Bank to lend directly to women in Bangladesh, taking on risks that other lenders would typically avoid while also innovating a support model that allowed for positive financial returns.[4] In U.S. markets, DBL Partners (at the time called Bay Area Equity Fund) managed a $75 million early-stage venture capital fund that invested in high-growth startups, including Tesla.[5] Despite the wide range of security types, risk and return targets, and impacts each investment firm was striving for, something in common connected them all and separated these strategies from other socially responsible investments and ESG funds. They were all attempting to have a social and environmental impact with their capital while also delivering some level of financial returns.

The Rockefeller Foundation was not the only organization that had begun to explore how these kinds of investments would further their charitable grants. W.K. Kellogg Foundation, JPMorgan Chase Foundation, MacArthur Foundation, and the Annie E. Casey Foundation were among the other early leaders. Additionally, a number of prominent family offices, including Mitch Kapor, Justin Rockefeller, Liesel Pritzker Simmons, Jeff Skoll, and Charlie Kleisner, were beginning to invest their personal wealth in this manner. Initially, these were mostly mission-oriented organizations and families committed to exploring the potential financial and social return of these strategies.

One issue the Rockefeller Foundation identified early was the need to accurately measure the impact of these kinds of investments. There was not enough data to categorize the myriad of approaches into likely outcomes. Still, the Rockefeller Foundation and some of the other early impact practitioners did have a common belief that sharing their learnings could create a broader market and crowd in more capital. Subsequent to the Bellagio convening, the Rockefeller Foundation created the Global Impact Investing Network (GIIN) to share learnings with the goal of educating the broader public about impact investing and advancing the various approaches.[6] Headed up by Amit Bouri, the first job of the GIIN was to bring definition and clarity to the impact investing space.

The Bellagio attendees also created, and the GIIN helped build consensus for, the following definition of impact investing: "Investing with the intention to generate measurable financial and social returns."[7] Since this early definition of impact investing has proved seminal to so much of the industry's subsequent work, it's worth dissecting the meaning of the three keywords to this novel and groundbreaking definition: *intention*, *generate*, and *measurable*.

Intentionality means an investor has an impact objective at the outset. Unfortunately, there are many examples of large asset managers claiming they have decades of experience and billions of dollars invested in impact, but these claims are made in retrospect as these firms had no impact strategy until recently. If you double-click to review the depth or magnitude of the impact they've created, there is little to show. This is because businesses that create meaningful impact require intentional, strategic decisions throughout their life.

Take a simple business like a grocery store. It's true that the grocer provides food, and that is at the very highest level of "good" for society, as we all need to eat. But the quality and price of the food and everything that goes into making it available can have a wide range of effects on its stakeholders. For example, does the grocery store prioritize an abundance of produce as you enter or strategically place sugary snacks? Is the produce, dairy, and meat sourced from industrial farms with questionable practices or local organic farms? How does the business owner treat its suppliers, and what quality of jobs are offered to their workforce? Is the business located in a food desert where access to basic food at an affordable price can change the quality of life for the community or in a high-income area that already has an abundance of options?

It's easy enough for an investor, in hindsight, to say that they are impact investors as the grocery store fed X million people. In reality, if they had had an impact intention from the start, the type of grocery store and how they managed it during the investment period would have differed significantly from a purely financially motivated investment decision. Every business has impact, both positive and negative, but intentionality sets impact-focused companies apart.

Generate speaks to an investor's involvement in the impact that is created. It's not enough to have exposure to businesses doing good; rather, the investor has to help in some way. *Additionality* is a technical term many in the industry use to describe this type of causal effect. Additionality could be through capital, especially if the impactful company may not have raised as much capital or at the same price had it not been for the impact investor. Or it could be through active engagement with the company to create value.

More typical value-add revolves around business strategy. For example, an investor could help a high-quality healthcare services company expand into areas with lower-income households. Another role I see investors play is holding companies accountable for their business practices, perhaps around ensuring equal access to the best jobs and professional development. Note how this form of active management is highly unlikely if the investor doesn't have the skillset for managing impact. For example, after the killing of George Floyd in 2020, there was a large wave of investment firms making statements of support for the Black community. However, many were skeptical of whether words might translate into action, knowing there were no resources, capabilities, or strategies behind these promises. They were right, and without this capability, these words fell flat.

Measurability is essential to assess the quality of impact. The field of measurement is developing quickly, and there are considerations of precision, practicality, cost, and quality that make for a range of approaches. We'll cover these in greater depth later in Chapter 10.

For now, it's important to understand how easy it is for investors to make false or exaggerated claims about impact if there is no measurement behind it. My favorite example is, "Ten million lives *touched*" in an impact report. What does that mean? Even worse, these same reports feature stock images of women or people of color graced by the help of a businessperson. And of course, it's printed on very heavy stock, glossy paper that will certainly be recycled (irony intended!). There is likely no real measurement happening in these investments, and that tends to go hand in hand with a lack of intentionality and a lack of active impact management.

If you see the thread, what matters most to be an impact investment is that there is an impact objective. Impact is not something to consider or evaluate. It must be a core reason alongside a financial return for making the investment. This is fundamentally what differentiates impact investing from ESG investing. The latter requires only consideration of impact factors but does not call for impact to be part of the objective for making the investment. My distinction here will become clearer when we cover ESG investing in greater detail in Chapter 3.

In addition to the core components of the GIIN definition, it is also important to denote what is *missing*: it lacks any specificity of how much or what type of financial and social return should qualify as an impact investment. This is not because impact investing requires a lower than typical financial return. The myth that somehow impact investments deliver less yield than a nonimpact investment is absurd, yet the myth persists due to impact's origins with nonprofit institutions. And yes, there are impact investments that provide a below-market return, but when done correctly, it is intentional to create a certain type of impact that otherwise wouldn't be possible if it weren't for the lower rate of return, and the trade-off is described in the objective up front.

The Omidyar Network, a $1.5 billion foundation and impact investment firm started by eBay founder Pierre Omidyar in 2004,[8] shared their framework for financial returns from impact investing in a white paper titled "Across the Returns Spectrum."[9] The Omidyar Network expects the same level of direct, company-level impact across its portfolio (Figure 1.2). However, Category A: Commercial Investments, are for companies with impact embedded in their business model, and commercial financial returns have already been market-validated or there is reason to believe it will be likely. Given the market validation, it's less likely that these investments will lead to what Omidyar refers to as *market impact*, which is the effect of accelerating the development of a market that reaches currently underserved or disadvantaged populations.

For example, Tesla, the electric vehicle manufacturer with a current market capitalization of roughly $750 billion,

Figure 1.2   The spectrum of returns

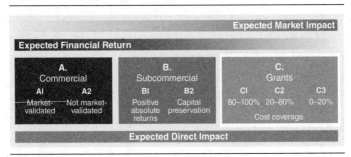

Source: Bannick, M., Goldman, P., Kubzansky, M., & Saltuk, Y. (n.d.). (rep.). Across The Returns Continuum (pp. 1–22). Omidyar Network.

was, earlier in its existence as a new privately held company, considered by many to be an impact investment because of the positive environmental outcomes its business would drive. While many nonimpact investors participated in early rounds of financing, so did impact funds such as DBL Partners, which was able to achieve competitive venture capital returns.

Category B investments are considered Subcommercial, in that Omidyar accepts lower financial returns in exchange for the promise of significant market impact. For example, companies launching businesses in new markets often need more time to overcome barriers and establish a profitable business model, potentially reducing the financial return for early investors. For those companies that are successful, however, future investments may fall in Category A.

For example, Mission Driven Finance manages a real estate investment trust (REIT) that expands access to quality childcare. By owning childcare properties and being a mission-aligned landlord providing stable leases for family-based childcare, Care Access Real Estate expands the supply of affordable childcare.[10] While the REIT may provide a lower return for investors than a similar REIT without an impact focus, it enables long-term resilience of these essential businesses and improves earnings for childcare providers, who are primarily women of color.

Category C investments are grants where the Omidyar Network does not expect to receive any capital back but does expect a high level of market impact. Specifically, Omidyar's thesis is that early grant capital will enable these organizations to become financially sustainable over time by being able to cover 80–100% of their costs through earned revenues. DonorsChoose.org is an example in Omidyar's portfolio.[11] This is an online marketplace where teachers and individual donors collaborate to bring students in U.S. public schools the resources they need to learn. Originally relying on grants from Omidyar to cover its operational expenses, DonorsChoose.org was eventually able to shift to a model in which it charges fees to donors who use the site.

The GIIN's definition also does not specify an asset class, a security type, or even a stage of business. The field did emerge first in early-stage venture capital but has expanded into all corners of the investment industry today, which we will cover in Part Two. There are compelling impact investments in small businesses, farms and forests, high-growth technology startups, century-old family-owned businesses, real estate, and public companies. Debt, equity, and everything in between is fair game. The approach to generating impact is unique to each asset class, and there are a range of expected outcomes. Investors who want to drive impact from their portfolios thus have the choice to do so across all of their investments, with different tools in their toolbox, or pick one or two asset classes that align most closely with their objectives.

The diversity of objectives and approaches to impact is what makes it powerful, fulfilling, and widely applicable to investors of all types. So why did it take so long to emerge as a viable investment strategy?

Chapter Two

Why Now? The Right Time for Creative Disruption

~

IF THE ROCKEFELLER FOUNDATION coined *impact investing* in 2007 and attempts to invest this way go back two decades further, why are we just now starting to see it adopted at scale by mainstream asset managers?

To answer this question, we need to step back from the investor's seat and consider impact investing as a noninvestment professional with a desire to improve quality of life. For some of us, this means understanding our privileges such as quality housing, time to pursue hobbies and passions, and access to resources such as education and healthcare.

I believe that everyone desires a world where more people can live with dignity, health, and opportunity. The disagreement lies in how to organize society's resources to achieve these goals, with some believing that minimal government involvement is the best way to incentivize people to earn a good life. Others see the challenges with that approach, recognizing that we don't all start with the same abilities and resources, so we should find ways to redistribute them in ways that are more equitable.

However, we can all agree that governments have yet to be able to address our needs as a society. News stories increasingly report how Gen Zers are living with angst about the effects of climate change, with some even questioning the viability of planning for a family in the future. But it's not just Gen Z that is stressed out. There is angst among Millennials, Gen Xers, and even Baby Boomers about how we as individuals or families will face these changes.

The rise of technology, which has created so much wealth, productivity, and possibility, also drives the malaise that affects every generation. For example, the use of social media and gaming has led to ever-increasing rates of loneliness, body-shaming, and loss of social skills for children and teens. Technology wields considerable personal autonomy and choice over learning, from online schools to coding boot camps, but also creates more uncertainty over how long your skills will last. This goes for whether you are an assembly-line worker competing against autonomous machines or a lawyer watching the rise of ChatGPT.

The feeling that "this moment is unique" is a common refrain in every generation. Yet, factually, so many uncertainties facing us today suggest that this moment in time—with all of the environmental, geopolitical, and social challenges we face—really is different. For the first time in U.S. history, it's more likely that children will grow into adults with a lower standard of living than their parents. This is not a doomsday scenario, and it does not mean the world as we know it is ending, but we are most certainly facing the reality that there are more variables at play and fewer reliable tools to achieve the kind of economic mobility that we all strive for and that prior generations have achieved in this country.

Casting a vote on election day doesn't give many people confidence that this is all we need to do to solve the monumental challenges facing our collective futures. Donating money every time there is a school shooting doesn't feel more impactful than making a social media post to send your thoughts and prayers. Paying $20 to offset your carbon emissions from your flight also feels more like an attempt by the airlines to pacify your climate fears than truly prevent the effects of extreme weather. Choosing to buy goods and services that were intentionally made with regard to the effect on workers and the planet, not just business owners, is perhaps the closest we get to feeling like we have any control over our fate.

U.S. households have more in savings or investable capital than they give away in philanthropy each year. We can use these resources to make change *now*. Philanthropic organizations such as the Heron Foundation have considered this, noting that the 5% given away each year to programs would be much more effective if they also tapped the 95% of capital in their endowment to further its mission and began doing so in 2012.[1]

Not all of these shifts have been led by institutions themselves. The public has also played an important role in forcing foundations to confront how a mismatch between what they were investing in with the 95% of the foundation's corpus and how that worked against the goals of the 5% of the mission-aligned capital.

Take the Gates Foundation, the largest in the world at $67 billion.[2] Following the IRS guidelines, as most foundations do, the Gates Foundation gives away at least 5% of its assets yearly to avoid taxes. That equates to donating roughly $3.35 billion to its main philanthropic focus areas of global health initiatives, public education in the United States, and social services in the Pacific Northwest where Microsoft is located.

But what about the other $63.65 billion? In 2007, the *L.A. Times* published a report about the alarming 95% portion of the Gates Foundation endowment that was invested in companies perpetuating the very challenges that the 5% was trying to fight.[3] Specifically, the article cited $218 million in grants toward polio and measles immunization and research worldwide, including the Niger Delta. At the same time, it had invested $423 million in five companies—Eno, Royal Dutch Shell, ExxonMobil, Chevron, and Total of France—primarily responsible for most of the flares blanketing the Niger Delta with pollution well beyond permitted amounts in the United States and Europe, where these companies also operated.

The *Times* reported that local leaders blamed oil development for fostering many of the afflictions that the foundation combats. For example, oil boreholes also fill with stagnant water, which is an ideal breeding ground to spread malaria, one of the key diseases that the foundation is fighting. Oil workers are also a magnet for prostitution, which contributes to a surge in HIV and teenage pregnancy, both of which the Gates Foundation targets to ease the ills of the poor.

The *Times* article had an explosive impact on the Gates Foundation and other U.S. foundations generally. Two days later, the Gates Foundation announced that it would review its holdings and approach to investments and explore other strategies to fulfill its social responsibility, both in terms of the foundation's aspirations and in understanding the impact it might have. In 2009, the foundation created the Strategic Investment Fund team to begin making nongrant investments to "address urgent challenges in global development, global health, and education."[4] After a $400 million pilot, it has grown to a $2.5 billion effort. Despite seeming like a large amount of money, it still translates into only a 4% allocation of the total foundation. However, I'm optimistic that success will lead to further growth. Moreover, the ripple effect of more foundations making similar shifts continues to create an impact.

Even government bodies are looking for better solutions. The United Kingdom created a Social Investment Task Force in 2000 to assess how the government could improve its capacity to create wealth, economic growth, and an improved social fabric in its poorest communities.[5] The task force members included experts from various fields, including Sir Ronald Cohen.

Often considered the godfather of venture capital in Europe, Sir Ronald cofounded Apax Partners in 1972.[6] This was one of Britain's first venture capital firms and was founded very early, even by U.S. standards. For reference, Sequoia was founded in the same year. Now, with $65 billion in assets under management, the firm has grown to become one of the largest global private investment firms.

In Sir Ronald's book, *Impact: Reshaping Capitalism to Drive Real Change,* he writes about getting into venture capital because of a desire to do good and do well at the same time.[7] This included job creation, but he also realized that venture capital was neither creating jobs for the poor nor solving the growing inequality gap at the time. When the U.K.'s Treasury wanted to deal with poverty by launching the Social Investment Task Force, they wanted to include private-sector innovators because they were concerned that however much money the government throws at social issues, it doesn't seem to make much progress.

One of the major accomplishments of the task force was the creation of Big Society Capital, a social investment bank. The bank was capitalized with £50 million each from Barclays, HSBC, Lloyds Banking Group, and the Royal Bank of Scotland, as well as £400 million reclaimed assets dormant in England's banking system. Initial investments included early-stage impact investment funds, social impact bonds, and an affordable office space for social enterprises and charities.[8] Having crossed the 10-year anniversary of the official launch of Big Society, the bank has helped catalyze more than £9 billion of investment in the U.K.'s social impact ecosystem. Moreover, more than 75% of the bank's capital is specifically invested in vulnerable communities in England.[9]

Then came the Global Financial Crisis in 2008, which called into question the sense of safety in our financial system. What other risks might jeopardize our portfolios if subprime mortgages could balloon into such a large risk to families and the entire system? It unleashed cryptocurrency adoption, as many lost trust in the U.S. dollar during the largest monetary stimulus in history.

Let's also not forget the bankruptcy of one of the United States' largest investor-owned electric utilities, Pacific Gas and Electric (PG&E), due to liabilities from California's wildfires. Oakland, California-based New Energy Nexus was created from the bankruptcy as an ecosystem of funds and accelerators to back diverse clean-energy entrepreneurs.[10] This event made it clear that our trust in markets for retirement savers to pensions is not free or clear from the multiple layers of uncertainty and risk presenting our society in the coming decades—and that our government alone isn't able to solve these crises.

One by one, entrepreneurial investors and change-makers began experimenting with approaches to driving impact. ESG management, or the incorporation of how a company manages its effects on various stakeholders, also rose during the past decade leading up to 2008. This created the necessary backdrop of acceptance from mainstream asset managers to begin understanding more proactive and targeted impact investment strategies.

In many ways, we are witnessing a return to what began in the 1960s with investors divesting from corporations deemed "bad actors." Divestment is a form of protest that resembles consumer boycotts, except in this case, the boycott involves selling stock. The most famous and perhaps effective was the "Divest South Africa" movement, which played a critical role in ending apartheid, a system of institutionalized racial segregation.

What began as student protests on college campuses led to the realization that the investment activities of university endowments can send powerful messages. With nearly half of the S&P 500 having some business in South Africa in the 1980s, students believed that a mass sale of these companies would get the attention of CEOs. No one wants to be in the press for contributing to racism. In fact, if enough investors sold, there was even a chance that the company's share price would be affected.

Hampshire College was the first to divest, and by 1988, there were 155 college endowments with some form of divestment effort.[11] This led to more significant movement— 90 cities, 22 counties, and 26 state pension funds at least partially divested from South African businesses. A similar momentum was occurring outside the United States as well.[12]

So, what effect did this have on apartheid? More than 200 U.S. companies eventually cut ties with South Africa, a $1 billion loss in American investment.[13] The flight of capital raised awareness of apartheid, sparking Congress to consider and eventually pass sanctions against the South African government. The local currency also faced devaluation and hyperinflation.

While it's hard to know exactly how much of an effect the divestment specifically had on ending apartheid in 1994, it certainly contributed to a ripple effect that led to the election of President Nelson Mandela, who had just spent 27 years in prison due to his involvement in the anti-apartheid movement. What made it effective, though, was the significant number of U.S. businesses operating in South Africa and how significant U.S. capital was to these businesses.

Many divestment movements came after South Africa. Some were focused on countries, including Sudan, due to its human rights violations. The instigators of divestment movements have often been students appealing to their university endowment officers, such as the ongoing fossil fuel divestment campaigns. Other groups with an informed view, such as the American Medical Association's campaign against tobacco companies, have also been attempted.[14] However, there has not been a divestment movement as effective as anti-apartheid.

One of the reasons the South Africa divestment movement was so successful was because of how coordinated it was. Perhaps not intentional at first, but the fact that university endowments, pensions, and religious investors were rowing in the same direction made it hard for corporate leaders and elected officials to ignore. This broad-based understanding of how investment portfolios can speak to an investor's mission also allowed the concept of ESG investing to take hold, creating the necessary backdrop for impact investing to rise.

Chapter Three

Hold On, What About ESG?

$\approx$

THIS IS A BOOK about impact investing, but as we just learned, impact investing also has roots in environment, social, and governance (ESG) investing. The two have distinct approaches, but impact investing requires some level of ESG assessment and management. This chapter aims to provide a deeper explanation of its theory and application before we move on and focus the rest of the book on impact investing.

It's a critical topic to understand because the ESG investment movement has faced significant pushback in recent years, both from advocates of corporations playing a role in social good and from those wholly opposed to the idea. Some of this is justified—the data and decision-making underlying ESG funds and ratings can often be shoddy and confusing—but this is not always true. No matter one's view, the ESG investment industry is a very large market. It currently represents somewhere between $30 and $40 trillion in assets under management globally, and despite some recent performance wobbles and drawdowns, that number is expected to grow to between $35 and $50 trillion by 2030.[1]

While ESG and impact investing share a similar view that corporations that are effective at managing their impact on various stakeholders will reduce risk and thus improve returns in the long run, their objectives and mechanisms to create positive impact are quite different. ESG investing looks to integrate the environmental, social, and governance practices of a company into the investment analysis but stops short of necessitating a measurable impact from the investment. In other words, the objective is not to drive impact through your investment but to consider the impact that would occur regardless of whether you invest. The theory is that if enough investors act in this way, corporations will be more likely to choose to have a positive impact to gain the interest of investors or avoid backlash from them.

This differs greatly from impact investors, who expect a direct positive impact from each investment.

This lack of direct impact is why many impact-supportive investors take issue with ESG and see impact investing as a necessary and much-needed corrective. "What is the point if there is no impact?" they ask, and follow up with worries of greenwashing, which is the opportunistic marketing of social or environmental benefits without substantial evidence. It's true that the top holdings in many ESG funds include Microsoft, GE, or even Royal-Dutch Shell, which makes it hard to see any difference between an ESG and a non-ESG fund.

We can debate ESG's merits as an impact investment strategy, but it is an important and growing concern to corporations. This is especially true for large, multinational businesses that are keen to impress consumers, regulators, investors, and employees with their ESG bona fides and actions. The rise of corporate social responsibility (CSR) roles at corporations to manage ESG data and questions from investors and the public is exactly why some believe that "woke capitalism" threatens democracy.

The trouble is that ESG has become a victim of its success and is now a lightning rod for politicians who don't fully understand it. The acronym is a catchall for every type of potentially socially good investment. In reality, it has developed into a risk management tool respected by the most sophisticated investors regardless of any impact objective.

How and why did this happen, and what should impact investors do with it?

In the early days, it was a simple and fairly intuitive way to denote some industries or companies as "bad" because of their negative effect on the environment and society. Most commonly included were the "sin" industries—tobacco, alcohol, gambling, and firearms. "Socially responsible investing," as it was called at the time, typically utilized negative screens to create portfolios free of whatever an investor wanted to screen out, offering investors a way to "do no harm."

But rather than focus on the "bad companies" and avoid highlighting the differences in everyone's personal beliefs, James Gifford and Paul Clements-Hunt at the United Nations Environment Program Finance Initiative (UNEP FI) and Georg Kell at the UN Global Compact had the brilliant idea of shifting the conversation to the potential value creation from effective management, or value destruction of mismanagement, of various issues. Environmental, social, and governance were simply three broad categories for communicating the potential issues that the UNEP FI discussed in their seminal report "Who Cares Wins" in 2004.[2] Since then, the acronym ESG has taken off as a less judgmental and more easily embraced term by the financial industry.

As the field grew more sophisticated, it evolved rigorously to consider the percentage of revenues a business might derive from these industries. For example, a pulp and paper manufacturer with significant customer concentration in Phillips Morris or an advertising business specializing in alcohol may be excluded from a portfolio. The list of activities or products deemed negative for society also grew to include nuclear weapons, pornography, fossil fuels, and others.

In the aftermath of the 2008 financial crisis, both institutional and retail investors have become more attuned to sustainability factors, and they got a further boost of interest in the post COVID-19 era. The development of public equities ESG strategies, which today is most commonly referred to as *ESG investing*, coincided with the advent of exchange-traded funds (ETFs), and the interest in these types of products has quickly come to dominate the marketplace. The fast-paced growth of the ESG marketplace led to a number of the criticisms we hear today.

Ironically, the birth of the ESG acronym in 2003 came from an attempt to move *beyond* any subjective view of what is good or bad for society and instead to help identify a range of business management practices that were once considered "nonfinancial" but are now seen as having a potentially material effect on strategy, revenues, expenses, and profits.

It is surprising to me that successful investors never thought these practices would have a financial effect. Just consider the legal liability from exposing employees to significant safety risks or the failure to account for an increase in flood or other climate-related risk as a result of climate change. The effect of several environmental, social, and governance factors could also play out against a corporation's brand reputation, impacting its stock price or its ability to attract and retain employees.

In hindsight, the choice of these three words—*environmental, social,* and *governance*—was perhaps so broad that it opened up the risk of criticism. For example, environmental considerations include how a company manages its waste to employee and community safety. Surely, counting plastic utensils in the company kitchen and whether a company knowingly pollutes the environment through risky manufacturing practices feel like two very different types and magnitudes of harm. Similarly, governance factors include everything from executive compensation to data privacy.

Fortunately, the understanding and analysis of ESG factors have grown more sophisticated over the years to make the link to financial performance clearer. Most notably, the Sustainable Accounting Standards Board (SASB) and International Sustainability Standards Board (ISSB) were created and subsequently consolidated under the IFRS Foundation in 2022.[3] The organization provides industry-specific guidance on the relevant ESG factors affecting enterprise value. The standards identify factors considered most relevant to financial performance across 77 industries, with an average of seven factors per industry.

These standards provide a baseline for companies to know what to manage rather than starting from the rather ambiguous and unending factors that could fall under environmental, social, and governance. Moreover, the standards were developed with a rigorous and transparent standard-setting process that included evidence-based research; broad and balanced participation from companies, investors, and subject-matter experts; and oversight and approval from an independent board. The standards are publicly available and updated regularly to incorporate the latest data and insights.[4]

ESG standards can be useful to businesses and investors. J.B. Hunt Transport Services is one of the world's largest supply chain companies and the first road transportation company to utilize SASB.[5] Facing risks and scrutiny about its climate impact from investors and other stakeholders, the company also saw an opportunity to address these challenges head-on and set an ambitious goal to reduce carbon emissions by 32% by 2034. Knowing where to start was a challenge, and utilizing the SASB standards helped the company to identify which key metrics to track, manage, and show progress. Today, J.B. Hunt is focused on incorporating alternative-powered equipment into its fleet, expanding the use of biogenic fuels, and improving fuel economy.

SASB helped the company identify other ESG factors, including worker safety, that are also worth managing closely due to their materiality to the business.

With evidence-based guidance on what corporations should manage to avoid costly risks, it's no surprise that executives have embraced ESG. The exponential growth of ESG assets under management only underscores the importance. It is no longer just mission-driven or socially responsible investors looking for companies managing ESG well, but some of the world's largest and most influential investors that want to avoid risks in their portfolios.

In March 2020, the chief investment officers of the world's three largest pension funds—the California State Teachers' Retirement System (CalSTRS), the Japanese Government Pension Investment Fund (GPIF), and the U.K.'s Universities Superannuation Scheme (USS)—penned a letter making the case that "if we were to focus purely on the short-term returns, we would be ignoring potentially catastrophic systemic risks to our portfolio" and that "asset managers that only focus on short-term, explicitly financial measures, and ignore longer-term sustainability-related risks and opportunities are not attractive partners for us."[6]

The letter urges their asset manager partners to "rethink their strategies and enhance their disclosures .... regarding their interactions with stakeholders, society, and the environment so that we can collaborate in generating and enhancing long-term value."

Note that the bar was set low to consider solely new strategies and disclose information. I think this was intentional, in part, to allow some of the largest asset managers in the world who managed their portfolios to take that first step toward ESG integration.

For investment firms seeking to include ESG factors in financial analysis, SASB's standards are often the first building block. Some investors utilize SASB's factors as a check-the-box risk management tool, while others go as far as to incorporate the disclosures into discounted cash flow models when determining a business's valuation. However, what comes next in utilizing this analysis in the investment process depends on the investor's objective. We can look at another important organization, the UN PRI, to gain perspective on the range of approaches.

In 2005, the then United Nations Secretary-General Kofi Annan gathered a group of the world's largest institutional investors to join a process to develop the "Principles for Responsible Investment."[7] This 20-person investor group came from large asset owners in 12 countries and was supported by a 70-person group of experts from the investment industry, intergovernmental organizations, and civil society. Together, they came up with six principles that PRI signatories would sign to pledge their commitment as an ESG investor.

Principle 1: We will incorporate ESG issues into investment analysis and decision-making processes.
Principle 2: We will be active owners and incorporate ESG issues into our ownership policies and practices.
Principle 3: We will seek appropriate disclosure on ESG issues by the entities in which we invest.
Principle 4: We will promote acceptance and implementation of the Principles within the investment industry.
Principle 5: We will work together to enhance our effectiveness in implementing the Principles.
Principle 6: We will each report on our activities and progress towards implementing the Principles.

Source: Principles for Responsible Investment. (n.d.). About the PRI. https://www.unpri.org/about-us/about-the-pri.

For investors fully committed to ESG, you can see a certain level of accountability beyond simply considering ESG factors. Principle 1 speaks to incorporating ESG into decision-making. Yet it was also strategic and essential for the UN to make clear that signatories will conduct these practices while also fulfilling their fiduciary responsibilities to include all investor types, from sovereign wealth funds to corporate pensions. With that bright line, in many ways, it made clear that these principles do not *require* anything different from an investor's objectives without an ESG mandate, continuing the confusion over whether ESG makes any difference.

Today, there are nearly 4,000 signatories with $120 trillion in assets under management. I can say for certain that only a small fraction of these would sign a pledge stating that their investment objective is to "generate measurable social and financial returns" as impact investors do.[8] In fact, GIIN signatories represent \$1 trillion of impact assets under management—less than 1% of PRI signatories' AUM.

Although impact investing and ESG investing have different objectives that have developed as different strategies and even industries, it's hard to believe that an impact investor can be great at generating impact if they aren't capable of analyzing and managing ESG factors. My professional journey as an impact investor, which we'll cover in the next chapter, began in the ESG industry and continues to inform my perspective on how to best manage impact risks. While we won't dive any deeper into best practices for ESG in this book, it is worth asking about and evaluating in any investor's portfolio.

Chapter Four

My Journey to Impact Investing

～

WHEN I BEGAN MY journey as an impact investor in 2004, I didn't expect it ever to become part of the mainstream vernacular or relevant to the Little Book investing book series. In fact, I remember Googling "businesses that do good" and struggling to find much more than advertisements for Ben & Jerry's ice cream and Stonyfield Farm's yogurt. I also could not trust it would be a financially stable career. And as an immigrant's child, it was made clear from the beginning that making money was the most important thing for me to become an adult.

My mother and father moved from India to the United States in the 1970s for better economic opportunities. Like most immigrants, they left behind their family, culture, and social status. It was only natural that they emphasized that education is strictly to secure a well-paying job and respect in the community. As the saying goes, children of Indian immigrants can be doctors, lawyers, or failures.

Yet, my parents set an example that created an even higher expectation for me. When I was seven years old, in addition to successful careers as a NASA engineer and corporate executive, they started and ran a nonprofit Ashram that provided free yoga, meditation, and spiritual programs. Taking the yogic path of selfless service, they eventually let go of maximizing financial gains to prioritize the Ashram. My parents took their savings and invested in a gas station that would financially fund the Ashram so that they could devote the vast majority of their time to teaching others for free.

This set the stage for my lifelong search for an answer to whether maximizing earnings and doing good had to be separate activities to do each well. As I came of age and understood how the world works, I could only see examples of the two-pocket strategy—do good in one pocket and earn a living in the other; never let the two goals mix. In the case of my parents, who were and still are my highest inspiration, did imparting the wisdom and practice of yoga offset all the gasoline and cigarettes they sold? Why wasn't there a way to do all the good work at the Ashram with a funding source aligned with the Ashram's mission? I wondered if one is generously philanthropic with their fortunes, is it morally acceptable to maximize wealth creation while potentially creating harm for others?

Of course, these aren't new questions. I was exploring an age-old dilemma for capitalism that goes back to even earlier than the U.S. robber barons of the nineteenth century. Is it enough to make your fortune in any way possible and then devote some part of that money to philanthropy? Or do we need to drive the whole engine of our economy toward good?

Taking it one step further, is a well-run society one in which businesses maximize profits for shareholders without consideration of other stakeholders, as long as the government and philanthropy can take care of the social and environmental costs? For decades, businesses poured toxic waste into lakes and rivers to maximize their profits, and taxpayers and people's actual health eventually paid the price. The same goes for child labor. The government often takes too long to course correct, and we all pay for that. As an economics student at Babson College, this "heads I win, tails you lose" approach seemed wildly inefficient to me. Capitalism can surely do better, right?

As a young entrepreneur who started several small businesses in my teens (boring yet profitable ones like website design and summer storage for college students, as well as my favorite, Priya's Apple Chips, where I sold dehydrated apples to highlight the flavor profiles of obscure varieties), I also wondered if there was a way to waste less time and energy to get to the same endpoint of financial security *and* contribute to society. Entrepreneurship is about making things—products, services, or processes—better. Had anyone considered using the tools of entrepreneurship to make capitalism better?

This pondering led to an independent study with a history professor. I studied the role corporations played in previous social movements and learned that investors are an underutilized key leverage point in this process. Yes, the government creates regulations and tax incentives to influence corporate behavior, consumers can boycott products sold by businesses doing harm, and some workers can even choose who they work for. Yet it struck me that investors, who can directly influence valuations and board decisions, were sorely underestimated. Learning about how critical stock divestments from corporations doing business in South Africa were in ending apartheid inspired me to wonder if the investment industry could one day be part of the solution.

Having realized that investors hold significant power, I next embarked on a project my senior year in college, interviewing money managers to understand how they were considering the potential effects of poor business management on the environment and laborers. Unfortunately, almost every conversation started and ended with the investment manager dismissing me. Perhaps it's because their time horizon for investing was too short to see how these factors might affect earnings or that they grew up in an era where you'd lose credibility if you even thought about the virtues of a business. Or maybe they weren't used to young women asking them tough questions?

There was one person who seemed to get it. Amy Domini started a mutual fund in 1991 that aimed to invest in "companies helping to create long-term value for people, planet, and profit."[1] What did she mean by this? Were Domini's investments really any different? As I dug into the mechanics of *determining* which companies are creating this value, I stumbled upon KLD Research & Analytics in Boston, Massachusetts, an investment research company started in 1989. The inception years of these firms were a long enough time ago that they must have answers, right?

KLD is most known for creating and managing the Domini 400 Social Index, a "do-gooder" version of the S&P 500, which Amy Domini's mutual fund was based on at the time. KLD also provided research on corporate behavior to other investors. With KLD's research database, you could access their ratings on a public company's treatment of employees, environmental stewardship, or governance practices. I couldn't believe that they had a business doing this, given how few money managers had any interest in this data. At the time, their clients were primarily financial advisors building portfolios for wealthy investors wanting their investments to align with their values. This early approach to excluding "bad" companies was labeled socially responsible investing (SRI), the precursor to ESG investing.

It took some convincing, but in 2005 KLD's Thomas Kuh hired me as a 20-year-old to use the firm's research and indices to build more products like the mutual fund Amy Domini managed. It was a bet that more investable financial products linked to KLD's research would move more capital than selling a subscription to our research database. Our efforts were well timed, with the early days of passive investing gaining steam and asset managers looking for more ideas for index funds. The most notable for us was iShares, where KLD's indices were used to create some of the earliest SRI ETFs. Many years later, MSCI bought KLD, as their research and indices proved valuable.

My next stop was joining Northern Trust, the Chicago-based $1 trillion asset management business, as a product manager focused on quantitative equities. No SRI jobs existed at firms like this at the time. What led me to a role like that was a curiosity about what it would take to get a traditional firm like Northern Trust to create an SRI investment product. It became clear to me that clients were the instigators, and meeting that demand simply offered the potential for more profits. It wasn't altruistic but further proof that the investment industry could be a major force for good. If the holders of capital, from individuals to institutions, aim to invest with a mission, investment managers will deliver solutions. With evidence of client demand in hand, my boss supported me in writing a business plan for the company to create our own SRI investment funds. This was around the time ESG was coined, and other mainstream asset managers were getting on the bandwagon.

The assets under management (AUM) for ESG funds were growing exponentially, yet I saw a big issue: very few ESG professionals had any finance or investing experience. And I was part of that problem. How could we claim to be investors for good if we weren't even good investors?

Recognizing my shortcomings, I went to get some finance chops and pursued my MBA from the University of Chicago Booth School of Business. What happened next was unexpected—it made me a disbeliever in the ESG products I had created. I realized that the approaches taken to assess corporate behavior at the time were too simplistic and unlikely to produce impact or strong financial returns. I worried ESG was a marketing gimmick, and I didn't want to be part of something I didn't believe was creating lasting change. I fairly quickly left my job at Northern Trust and the fledgling ESG industry and did a 180—I set out in the hedge fund industry to gain practical investment skills and continue my search for a way to marry the objectives of money and good.

I wound up at Aurora Investment Management, a Chicago-based $14 billion fund of hedge funds. After nearly a decade at Aurora, I left to join a single-family office as their chief investment officer. At both firms, being an allocator to investment funds allowed me to understand multiple investment strategies across asset classes and observe the common thread for what makes an excellent investor and a viable investment strategy. It also gave me an important window into how company management teams interact with and are influenced by investors. Perhaps most importantly, it deepened my understanding of how asset owners operate and their role in influencing investment managers.

I didn't have an explicit mandate to create impact in those roles, but the professional experiences were informing my personal investments that aimed to drive positive change. While it was quite experimental at the time, I was curious to find investment strategies—from private loans to community projects to angel investments in startups with a social mission—that would appeal to my (now higher) investment standards while also having conviction about the depth of impact beyond what I saw in ESG funds. Even better would be to find situations where meaningful impact could make for a competitive advantage and, thus, strong returns.

Impact Engine was one of my personal investments long before I joined as chief investment officer and partner in 2018. When the firm started in 2012, we had no track record—financially or impact-wise. However, we were surrounded by successful investors, entrepreneurs, and CEOs willing to take the chance with their own capital to see if early-stage venture capital investments in impactful companies could deliver the holy "double bottom line." Today, we manage $250 million across venture capital and private equity strategies and are one among a growing list of reputed institutional investment firms fully committed to generating financial returns and impact.

I'm excited to share more with you about what we and our peers have learned over the past decade-plus of investing with an alignment between profits and purpose. In many ways, we built the ship at sea as there weren't models of success for us to follow before setting sail. We haven't figured everything out yet, but the next generation of impact investors is actively building off our approaches and disrupting the very nature of the investment industry as we know it. It's capitalism at its best.

What was meant to be a senior-year project to understand the relationship between corporations and social change ended up as a now 20-year career as an institutional investor. It turned out that I love investing, even if I went into this industry without any interest in it. The exciting thing is that the potential to invest with a mission brings more people to the table. There are many reasons why the finance industry is underrepresented by women, people of color, and other statistically less privileged identities, and I would add its lack of purpose—until now—as an important one.

Five years ago, Chicago Booth asked me to join the adjunct faculty to teach a course on impact investing. As one of the most prestigious business schools in the world, with a reputation for the most rigorous finance program, it was the ultimate sign that the investment industry was changing. Demand from clients is now being met by a supply of talent, and only good can come from that as these young professionals take impact investing to the next level. Much of what follows in Part Two and Part Three of this book is the theoretical and practical playbook that I share with my students each year. But first, we need to finish the story about how impact investing, despite many challenges for the asset management industry, became what it is today.

Chapter Five

How Impact Investing
Grew Up

ONE OF THE REASONS it took me so long to be a full-time, career impact investor was that it wasn't much of an industry until recently. When I graduated college in 2004, there were only a handful of jobs at SRI mutual funds. However, family offices and foundations were pioneering impact investing, which I describe as the experimentation phase (Figure 5.1). Today, we are in the codification stage of the industry's development, where there are a more significant number of impact investment firms. My perspective on

Figure 5.1 Stages of development for the impact investing field Courtesy of Parrish

	Experimentation	Early Adoption	Acceptance	Codification	Integration
	2000–2007	2007–2015	2016–2019	2020–2029	2030+
	Pioneering family offices and foundations innovate strategies for driving impact	Pure-play impact investment firms launch funds to prove strategies can perform	Mainstream firms launch impact funds with limited expertise, creating interest and confusion	Diversity of impact approaches and expected outcomes is understood and expected	Investors can easily identify and evaluate risk-return-impact dimensions in their portfolios and fully incorporate into asset allocation

Skoll, Rockefeller, and other family offices give credibility to effort

Impact Engine launches $525K accelerator

TPG raises $2B Rise Fund

Impact funds grow 40% over last two years, hitting $1 trillion

Impact Funds in Market & IAUM

these development stages comes from observing how other investment paradigms went through parallel phases. For example, value investing began with experimentation (e.g. Graham and Dodd) and then early adopters (e.g. Warren Buffet); next we saw acceptance (i.e. proliferation of value mutual funds), codification (e.g. Russell Value Indices), and finally integration (i.e. value factor investing). It's helpful to understand each of these stages for impact investing to better understand where the industry might be headed.

In the early days, the Rockefeller Foundation and other pioneering family offices and foundations were willing to use their capital to experiment to see what types of financial returns and social change could be possible. Other important investors included the MacArthur Foundation and Skoll Foundation even before there was an impact label or a designated allocation in their portfolios.

Early signs of success and a deeper understanding of possible potential outcomes led to the industry's early adoption period, where private investment firms were created to take in outside capital. SJF Ventures had a mission to create quality jobs in low-income communities through venture capital investments in sustainable industries.[1] Jonathan Rose Companies focused on affordable housing.[2] Microvest was one of the earliest private credit funds with a goal of financial inclusion and poverty alleviation.[3]

Impact Engine was also started during this period, initially as an accelerator program for social entrepreneurs. Still relatively new at the time, the idea behind startup accelerators was that in exchange for equity ownership, guidance, and support early in a venture's life can help accelerate a company's growth and increase its likelihood of success. Among the most well-known programs are Y Combinator, founded in Silicon Valley in 2005, and TechStars, founded in Boulder, Colorado, in 2006. While these programs posted successful financial results, they were not set up to evaluate or support a company's growth with an impact objective.

One of the first questions asked of early impact investment firms like Impact Engine was, "What kind of impact are you trying to create?" If you recall from the Global Impact Investing Network (GIIN) definition, impact is broadly defined as "social or environmental." Early leaders were Bridges Fund Management, which Sir Ronald Cohen, Michele Giddens, and Philip Newborough formed in 2002 to focus on reducing inequality through investments in poor communities in England.[4] Their inaugural £40 million venture capital fund was supported by the U.K. Social Taskforce discussed in Chapter 2. Others, like the Global Environment Fund, established in the 1990s, focused on preventing climate change.

While few would argue that reducing inequality or climate change is not impactful, these are not every investor's priorities. The divergent and diverse impact goals challenged the asset management industry. Without gaining enough consensus to attract many investors, impact funds were too small to be feasible or interested in offering these products.

For example, Impact Engine's first accelerator fund in 2012 was a whopping $525,000. Each startup received $25,000, leaving $325,000 to cover all the expenses of a 10-week program, demo day, and post-program support for these fledgling entrepreneurs. Let's state the obvious—there was very little compensation for the team. How many investors would be willing to take a massive pay cut to participate in this field, and why would the likes of KKR or Bain be interested in such an offering if they could not drive significant profits for their firm?

The industry needed a standard, a definition that could bring investors with disparate priorities together to increase capital allocated to the space. They found a solution in the Sustainable Development Goals (SDGs). This set of 17 goals (Figure 5.2) was developed at the United Nations Conference on Sustainable Development in Rio de Janeiro in 2012 and finalized by the UN in 2015.[5]

The SDGs were not designed for impact investors but rather to create a set of universal goals that meet the environmental, political, and economic challenges facing our shared society. While every country faces its unique challenges, the objective of the SDGs was to unite government leaders around issues that affect everyone to promote collaboration on solutions.

For impact investors, the SDGs presented an opportunity to establish a consensus about what social and environmental issues matter most. One hundred ninety-three members of the United Nations, believing these are universal goals that will

Figure 5.2   Sustainable Development Goals

Source: United Nations Department of Public Information. (n.d.). (rep.). Sustainable Development Goals Guidelines for the use of the SDG Logo, including the colour wheel, and 17 icons (pp. 1–75).

make all countries and societies better off, cuts through any debate. Moreover, the goals are broad and inclusive enough to provide a real investable opportunity set.

While each of the 17 goals is unique and many are independently large market opportunities, several are quite interconnected. Providing clean water and sanitation will contribute to good health and well-being; sustainable cities and communities are essential to taking climate action. This allows for impact fund managers to target one or a few SDGs to create a large enough investment universe to make money, drive measurable impact, and be financially viable.

The other holdup for mainstream finance to embrace impact investing was the worry about what achieving "impact" might do to financial returns. Tasha Seitz, one of my partners at Impact Engine, was part of our firm's investment committee from day one, as we wanted someone with a strong investment acumen to weigh in. She was previously a partner with JK&B Capital, a technology venture capital firm based in Chicago with $1.1 billion dollars under management. One of the key questions that Tasha had to consider was how the impact intentionality of each company would affect the addressable market, profit margins, go-to-market strategy, talent attraction, and other key success factors. This assessment centered around a goal of investing to prove that impact can reinforce a return-generating strategy. Over time, we learned which business models do indeed support this dual goal and make for a compelling investment strategy.

As the large variety of impact goals was consolidated and more proof points of strong financial performance were coming out of the first cohort of impact funds, large asset managers began to take notice. Bain Capital launched its inaugural impact fund, dubbed Bain Double Impact, in 2016 with a $250 million fundraise. TPG's Rise Fund topped that at $2 billion! Seeing firms with proven financial track records launch impact funds opened up the gate of acceptance by investors of all motivations, not just those who cared about impact.

The trouble was, it also began to create confusion in the market. What is the difference between TPG's impact fund and its non-impact fund? Were the SDGs just a convenient label to slap on, or was something actually different? For example, look at a common SDG targeted by these firms: "SDG 3: Good health and well-being." At a high level, every healthcare company in the world should contribute to this goal, right? But let's look more specifically at what the United Nations targets for SDG 3[6]:

3.1. Maternal mortality
By 2030, reduce the global maternal mortality ratio to less than 70 per 100,000 live births.

3.2. Neonatal and child mortality

By 2030, end preventable deaths of newborns and children under five years of age, with all countries aiming to reduce neonatal mortality to at least as low as 12 per 1000 live births and under-5 mortality to at least as low as 25 per 1000 live births.

3.3. Infectious diseases

By 2030, end the epidemics of AIDS, tuberculosis, malaria and neglected tropical diseases, and combat hepatitis, waterborne diseases and other communicable diseases.

3.4. Noncommunicable diseases

By 2030, reduce by one third premature mortality from noncommunicable diseases through prevention and treatment, and promote mental health and well-being.

3.5. Substance abuse

Strengthen the prevention and treatment of substance abuse, including narcotic drug abuse and harmful use of alcohol.

3.6. Road traffic
By 2020, halve the number of global deaths and injuries from road traffic accidents.

3.7. Sexual and reproductive health
By 2030, ensure universal access to sexual and reproductive healthcare services, including for family planning, information and education, and the integration of reproductive health into national strategies and programmes.

3.8. Universal health coverage
Achieve universal health coverage, including financial risk protection, access to quality essential healthcare services, and access to safe, effective, quality and affordable essential medicines and vaccines for all.

3.9. Environmental health
By 2030, substantially reduce the number of deaths and illnesses from hazardous chemicals and air, water and soil pollution and contamination.

Very clearly, the primary focus of SDG 3 is the population of citizens who cannot access quality healthcare. An impact fund claiming to focus on SDG 3 but is uninterested in investing in companies that serve families on Medicaid or those in developing countries should be scrutinized.

Those of us who had been thinking critically for many years about what makes for a high likelihood of deep, enduring impact and financial returns had answers but were not as big and well-known as these firms. Field builders like Impact Engine had to talk about our approaches—not just about what makes a business impactful but also how you can invest in impact and generate strong returns. This knowledge share marked the beginning of the codification stage, when the many different ways of being an impact investor become better understood versus lumped together. This is an important step for investors to know what to expect for their investments. Returning to the GIIN's definition of impact investing, neither the financial nor social return is set in stone. It's about having an objective and strategy for both and then being held accountable. This breadth of acceptable strategies creates a greater need for understanding specific approaches.

For Impact Engine, two important realizations drove our firm's core impact investment framework. Our first principle is that if you want to generate market rate returns, you must invest in large markets. This observation should be obvious to any *trained* investment professional familiar with Modern Portfolio Theory. According to Harry Markowitz's seminal research in 1952, a return-maximizing investor should hold a diversified portfolio of investments. Imposing any constraints to what can be invested in will lead to a suboptimal balance of risk and return. Impact investors, which focus on a subset of companies deemed impactful, knowingly constrain their investment universe. However, any *experienced* investor also knows that teams with specialized knowledge and focus, perhaps on a sector, can and do outperform even though the investment universe is constrained. Finding the balance between these two philosophies is essential.

Impact Engine followed this principle by selecting three of the largest social problems that are commercial opportunities for corporations: environmental sustainability, economic opportunity, and health equity. Together, these domains offer the potential to capture enormous societal needs, including the following:

- 90% of the global working population must be re-skilled by 2030. Failing to meet this demand could cost up to $15 trillion in lost GDP.[7]
- 1 in 3 U.S. adults forgo physician-recommended treatment due to cost.[8]
- More than 1.4 billion adults globally remain unbanked.[9]

Our second principle picked up where the first principle left off, which is to answer the question of what characteristics of a company will make its impact significant and enduring.

After analyzing our portfolio, those of our peers, as well as the large data set from environment, social, and governance (ESG) mutual funds and exchange-traded funds (ETFs), it was clear that a company's core product or service is the most powerful lever within a business model to create impact. Companies offering products and services that directly create positive impact benefit from a reinforcing tie between revenues and social good. Since customers purchase the company's product based on its efficacy, management teams are incentivized to continuously strengthen and demonstrate the impact of their products, and the impact cannot be easily decoupled if the company were to be acquired. We started calling this approach *product-based impact*. In Chapter 9 we will cover the four other "Ps" for business model impact strategies—place, people, process, and paradigm.

Product-based impact limits the investment universe, as not all industries offer goods and services that contribute positively to society, and not all companies in "beneficial industries" offer products with proven impact. So there is a paradox in our two principles and also why it takes quite a bit of skill to consider the implications of an inherently narrower universe of opportunities while looking for opportunities to expand. In fact, the second principle reinforced our conclusion that a market-rate impact investor must focus on large market opportunities.

With this key development and the industry's growing acceptance, Impact Engine grew into a $250 million asset manager with venture capital and private equity strategies that meet the expectations of institutional investors while also investing in companies that do drive impact. We measure this impact and report it to our investors alongside traditional financial performance reporting.

We couldn't have started Impact Engine the way we operate it today simply because the industry wasn't big enough. The other barrier that Impact Engine and all impact investment firms faced early on was that we were new. Even without an impact goal or approach, the number of investors willing to back a new investment firm is small. The hoops you have to jump through to earn these investors' trust are numerous and often reserved for those with privileged networks and identities. So if impact investing is new, by definition all impact investment firms are also new. Early backers of the first cohort of impact investment firms deserve so much credit for catalyzing what the $1 trillion and growing industry is today.

The premise of impact investing is simple—companies that can solve society's greatest problems are likely to be worth a lot of money. Yet the challenges posed in the pursuit of this goal have kept the industry from catapulting into a mainstream investment strategy for decades. Impact Engine is not the only firm that has successfully scaled, as there are many other investment firms with unique and compelling approaches that are also reaching scale. This helps usher in the Integration stage, when investors can fully identify and make decisions based on return, risk, *and* impact. The goal is not that every investment is an impact investment but rather that we can understand the impact of every investment.

Chapter Six

Who Can Be an Impact Investor?

NOW THAT WE KNOW the basics of impact investing, it's fair to ask to whom is this relevant? The answer is, all investors are impact investors—positively or negatively. This is because all investments have an impact beyond a financial gain or loss for the investor. It's not just investments in companies that make an impact through their products and services, the treatment of employees, or their carbon footprint. Your investment in a savings account funds bank loans, which could be to a local small business or a fossil fuel company.

Investors are usually unaware of the various funds and accounts in which their money is invested, let alone what type of impact those investments have. Understanding what you already own is the first step to becoming an intentional impact investor. You can then determine what changes or new investments align more with your objectives.

Starting with individuals, there are a range of objectives and potential impact investments. Many families simply want to align their investments with their values. This includes people across the political spectrum, from those opposing abortion to those seeking stricter gun control. Many individuals also care deeply about societal needs and innovations. In just the past year, I've come across impact funds focused on psychedelics for medicinal usage, biotechnology and healthcare services for cancer patients, and even space technology. I've found that if a strong case can be made for financial returns and impact that matters to them, individuals are open to including these investments in their portfolios.

Many of these investments are limited to wealthy people who meet the U.S. Securities and Exchange Commission (SEC) requirements for an accredited or qualified investor. This includes venture capital and private equity funds, as well as the possibility of being an angel (very early) investor directly into companies. While it's also possible to make intentional impact investments from your 401k or retail taxable account, there are limitations to the type of impact created in these products.

Many mutual funds or exchange-traded funds (ETFs) marketed as sustainable or impact investing align to certain themes but do not necessarily invest in companies with strategies focused on making an impact. For example, the $900 million Domini Impact Equity Fund invests 80–95% of its capital in companies that demonstrate "peer-relative environmental and social leadership" and only 5–20% in "solution-oriented companies" supporting the following themes[1]:

- Accelerating the transition to a low-carbon future
- Contributing to the development of sustainable communities
- Helping ensure access to clean water
- Supporting sustainable food systems
- Promoting societal health and well-being
- Broadening financial inclusion
- Bridging the digital divide and expand economic opportunity

It's not that Domini doesn't want to invest more in solutions, but there are not enough public companies with this focus in which to invest. As impact venture capitalists continue to fund high-impact companies that go on to the public market, we'll start seeing more options for retail impact investors. In the meantime, growing balances at funds like Domini demonstrate to the market that there is demand for high-impact companies, which I believe creates a positive effect.

There are also banking options that can have a more direct impact. Self-Help Credit Union is an example of a community development financial institution that could be an alternative for your checking or savings account. It was chartered in 1983 to partner with working families and communities often underserved by the financial marketplace, including people of color, women, rural residents, and low-income households. Its network has provided $10.9 billion in financing to borrowers to buy homes, start and grow local businesses, and strengthen community resources.[2] Amalgamated Bank is another example of a bank with a long history of providing affordable access to banking, supporting immigrants and affordable housing, and being a champion of workers' rights.[3] More recently, First Women's Bank was founded in 2021 as the only women-founded, women-owned, and women-led commercial bank in the country with a strategic focus on the women's economy.[4]

Opportunities also exist in short-term fixed-income products. For as little as $20, Calvert Impact Capital allows investments in its Community Investment Notes, a portfolio of loans to critical community and environmental needs around the world. This includes organizations and projects related to affordable housing and sustainable agriculture, for example. Since 1995, Calvert has made more than 1,000 loans to more than 550 organizations across 100+ countries and measures the impact of these investments.[5] Similar to a certificate of deposit (CD), the duration ranges from 1 to 5 years with interest rates up to 5%.

Intergenerational wealth management offers another juncture to pursue impact investments. As wealthy Baby Boomers transfer assets at unprecedented rates in the coming years, it has sometimes proven to be a real source of difficulty to get their children to take interest in managing their money. What I've found during my time managing a single family office and getting to know many other private offices is that including investments in areas that speak to the next generation's interests is an effective way to get them involved. It allows them to express their values with their dollars and brings their attention to the details necessary to make informed decisions about how their wealth should be managed.

Let me share a story about a friend to illustrate how adding an impact objective can solve this challenge. She is passionate about regenerative agriculture, even operates an urban farm, and sells produce at farmers' markets. I didn't know about the wealth she would inherit until she asked me if their family could invest in a way that addressed climate change. I, of course, answered yes and was excited to help her advocate for this possibility.

After my friend's passion areas were integrated into her family's investment strategy and portfolio, she went from having little knowledge of how to balance a budget to joining their family foundation's investment committee. I can repeat this story for another friend who is passionate about civic engagement and democracy building, and so on. In each of these cases, incorporating the younger generation's values and passion into the investment process truly transformed their relationship with money and their family.

Both family foundations and large private foundations have also played an important role in the growth of impact investing, and the opportunity is ripe for these investors. Every foundation has a stated mission, whether it be poverty alleviation, conservation, children's health, or even a geographic cause, such as supporting education programs in rural or urban areas. Carrying out this mission is paramount to maintaining its tax-exempt status as a 501(c)(3). Much effort goes into evaluating programs to support financially that further the mission, yet the IRS requires that only 5% of a foundation's endowment to be used for grants each year.

In the last few decades, several thoughtful foundation leaders began to consider how the other 95% of their assets are furthering their mission (or not). My favorite story is that of the F.B. Heron Foundation. Founded in 1992 with a mission to help people and communities help themselves, the foundation's endowment benefited greatly from the bull market in the 1990s. As its asset base soared, however, it also became clear to the organization's leaders that the rising markets did not translate into tangible benefits to the communities it sought to help in the same way.

During a board meeting in 1996, Heron's directors spent hours reviewing an investment manager's performance that affected the performance of 95% of its corpus but left little time to review whether the grants made out of the 5% mission-aligned part of the foundation's assets had been successful in furthering the mission. This realization on the part of the board led to their desire to evaluate the foundation's overall effectiveness. This led them to question whether Heron should be more than just a private investment company that uses its excess cash flow for charitable purposes. In fact, they could find little difference between how Heron operated and how a private investment company would operate if it used all of its profits for charitable purposes. What they ultimately determined was that the foundation's tax-exempt status and mission were indeed not driving the key decisions and activities of the organization. And they believed this should change.

Based on this determination, the board began considering not just the 5% payout requirement for 501(c)(3)s, but also the 95% of assets when making decisions about Heron's mission. As a next step, the board asked Heron's staff to explore "mission-related" investment strategies from the endowment to maximize the foundation's impact in low-income communities.

This happened slowly, and it required significant organizational change, including training investment staff on evaluating social impact from its portfolio and bringing on new team members with this type of expertise. It was far from certain how far the foundation would be able to go with leveraging its endowment portfolio to advance its mission. But the board continued to encourage an incremental approach to change, learning lessons along the way while striving to do better than the status quo for philanthropy.

Much like Rockefeller, Heron did find a few investment managers that today would be called impact fund managers. And within a decade, Heron's impact investing activity had grown to roughly 40% of its overall endowment, including everything from taxable municipal bonds to venture capital. In 2012, the foundation underwent a strategic review and decided to align 100% of its assets to its mission.[6] However, 2012 was still the early years for the impact investing ecosystem, and Heron soon discovered how hard it would be to achieve this goal while not altering other aspects of the portfolio's needs, like a certain asset allocation or liquidity profile. Despite these challenges, Heron has been a critical investor in supporting new managers and building the field, which today is able to support Heron and many other mission-driven investors.

University endowments are another investor that might have similar objectives as a foundation endowment. Funded by charitable donations, endowments hold permanent capital that funds a college's mission. This might include financial aid and scholarships, tuition increases, scientific research, faculty chairs or professorships, athletics, or even local community support. There is a balance between using the returns from the endowment in the operating budget, typically with a 5% annual payout, while taking a long-term investment time horizon to maximize returns.

Led by student activists, there is a long history of pressure put on endowments to consider the impact of its investments. Unfortunately, far fewer university endowments are making impact investments than we see among foundation endowments. The nonprofit Intentional Endowment Network (IEN) makes the case that $650 billion in endowment assets and $890 billion in university retirement funds serving 20 million students a year in the United States should provide an example to the future leaders and professions they serve.[7] For example, the students and faculty/staff retirees are also impacted by the potential negative impact of climate change if they don't play their part in mitigating it.

While it may seem like a pension is the furthest candidate to be an impact investor, there is a commonality between the case IEN is making and those advocating for pensions to invest with impact make. Let's consider that a pension serves the needs and interests of pensioners, including retired teachers or police officers. It's clear to most that those needs include the ability to pay out a monthly pension check to ensure their expenses can be paid. However, retirees on fixed incomes face the challenge of rising costs. Does it not follow then that it may be in the interests of pensioners to invest in companies that might reduce the costs of our healthcare system? How about the rising costs of housing or even housing insurance due to climate risks? While it may seem indirect, impact investments can meaningfully address a range of pensioners' needs and thus warrant the attention of trustees and asset managers involved in managing these pools of capital.

This does not mean that impact should be the only or primary objective when managing pension funds. Instead, there should be an intentional effort to evaluate where and how impact relevant to the pensioners can be generated while still meeting the financial return targets and staying within risk and liquidity constraints. This is an important nuance, as the Department of Labor made a ruling in 2022 that pension fiduciaries (those responsible for managing a pension plan) may—but not must—consider ESG factors when making investments when relevant to risk and return analysis.[8] This essentially allowed those considering ESG in decisions to be free and clear but not force all pensions to do it. This confusing ruling has been challenged in court several times, and it may not be the last we hear of it.

There are many other types of asset owners, from sovereign wealth funds to insurance companies. For board members and trustees, as well as investment teams or advisors serving these organizations, it is worthwhile to reexamine the core objectives of investing and see if and how impact can be added to the mix. Returning to the GIIN's definition, there is room for various financial and impact objectives. There is thus no reason to consider the impact only for certain types of investors or pools of capital. As we'll explore in Parts 2 and 3, incorporating impact investing has potential financial benefits. And at the very least, it helps investment teams find a greater and deeper perspective, uncover hidden risks and opportunities, and gain a greater sense of purpose.

Before we dive into the deep end of how to be an impact investor, I want to introduce you to a few other friends who help round out the picture of the motivations and skill sets that are building this industry.

Chapter Seven

Other Roads to the Same Place

———————— ❧ ————————

Today, people and institutions around the world are impact investors. They can range from individuals seeking a more impactful outcome for their retirement savings to millionaires and billionaires wanting to do more with their money beyond philanthropic giving. Impact investors also include foundations and endowments seeking to align the investments of their corpus with their core values and sovereign wealth funds and pensions, thinking about the future of their citizens and pensioners.

Behind each asset owner are professional investment managers and advisors who had to figure out how to deliver an impactful financial product. Before they had to figure out *how* to do it, they had to decide that it was worth doing. Learning about everyone's journey to become an impact investor is one of my favorite things about being part of this industry. It's often a story of someone's multiple identities coming together, a realization that they don't need to compartmentalize their values from their work. You can see the feeling of joy on their faces when they share their "aha" moment. I want to try to bring some of that to life for you, as it'll set the backdrop for understanding what these impact investors are after.

Going All-In on Impact: Jessica Droste Yagan

My partner and CEO at Impact Engine, Jessica Droste Yagan, started off thinking that governments and nonprofits were the only sectors for social change (and accordingly studied public policy at Haverford College). After reading "The Competitive Advantage of Inner Cities" in *Harvard Business Review* in her senior year, she instead leaned into a lifelong passion for leveraging capitalism for social good. She quickly shifted from a think-tank job offer in Washington, DC, to starting her career at the Initiative for a Competitive Inner

City (ICIC), a nonprofit founded by Michael Porter, the Harvard Business School professor who had authored that impactful paper and was known for "Porter's Five Forces." He created ICIC to bring that paper to life, with a mission to drive economic prosperity in America's inner cities through private-sector investment to create jobs, income, and wealth for local residents.[1]

Jessica went on to pursue her MBA at Stanford and her MPA at Harvard Kennedy School, with the goal of diving deeper into the intersection of business and social impact. After graduating with a dual degree that could take her in several directions to do good for the world, she landed at McDonald's. Yes, the restaurant chain is criticized for everything from causing obesity to its poor treatment of its employees. However, she saw the potential to make change in the world, moving the needle incrementally at what is one of the largest buyers of nearly everything it procures, from beef to straws. Jessica intentionally worked to create a role focused on the supply chain where she could create sustainable sourcing strategies. She learned many lessons there, including how to find win-win opportunities for business and society. For example, to protect the resiliency of the coffee supply chain, she led the launch of technical training programs for Central American coffee farmers so they could reduce disease, improve quality, and generate more income.

Jessica and I met through Impact Engine. She was among the first investors in 2012. She was immediately interested in putting her personal capital to work in a way that was aligned with her beliefs about the positive potential of capitalism. While Jessica never intended to become a career impact investor, investing in Impact Engine made her realize that her wealth was an untapped opportunity to support companies using their resources for good. She and her husband, a successful entrepreneur, eventually decided to work toward shifting all of their capital, including their family foundation endowment, to invest with an impact lens.

Investing with 100% impact was an ambitious goal, as it involved changing everything in their portfolio, from cash to private equity. It involved firing their wealth manager, who wouldn't take the goal seriously, and finding one that could bring equal rigor to both impact and financial returns.

Along the way, Jessica joined several membership organizations geared toward supporting families and foundations to move their investments toward positive impact. That included the ImPact, a global community of families with similar goals of aligning their wealth with their values to learn from others. Founded by Justin Rockefeller, Liesel Pritzker Simmons and Ian Simmons, and the Scodro Family, there are more than 70 member families across 20+ countries today.[2] Jessica is now on the board of directors at the ImPact and is an example to many of how she and her husband have shifted their assets.

As CEO of Impact Engine, Jessica manages many of our firm's business aspects, from fundraising to operations. I think that many of our investors are inspired by and gain confidence in seeing Jessica believe so much in impact investing that her dollars and entire career are aligned with it.

Using Private Capital for Public Good: Martin Nesbitt

Marty Nesbitt's journey took him from private investing to the public sector before realizing the powerful intersection between the two. After a successful career as a real estate investor, Marty founded and was CEO of the Parking Spot, the first nationally branded airport parking company, which he grew into a business worth more than $1 billion. Always drawn to public service, Marty also served as a board member to several public sector organizations, including serving as the Chairman of the Chicago Housing Authority. However, when his longtime friend, Barack Obama, announced his candidacy for President of the United States in 2007, Marty became campaign treasurer. He spent years weathering the campaign trail for both elections and became Chairman of the Barack Obama Foundation in 2014.

Having deep experiences in both the public and private sectors, Marty could appreciate the strengths of each. He developed a belief that larger societal issues like income disparity and health inequity could be addressed by leveraging the positive attributes of both the public and private sector. Marty also saw a financial value proposition at the intersection of the two that he felt was not recognized in the marketplace. He came to believe that companies that create societal value should be worth more to buyers.

Marty and his business partner, Kip Kirkpatrick, started private equity firm the Vistria Group in 2013 to invest in companies that are aligned at the intersection of public and private interest.[3] The Vistria Group believes that investing at this intersection creates both societal and economic value and believes that the industries where this impact could be the greatest are healthcare, education, and financial services. In forming a team, Marty and Kip recruited not just talented private equity professionals but also policy experts and operators in these industries to help their companies navigate the challenges and opportunities to create societal and economic value. People who have served at the highest levels of government and other career policy makers have been a part of The Vistria Group journey.

The Vistria Group recently celebrated its 10th anniversary, noting in its annual impact report that its thesis of generating market-leading financial returns alongside positive impact at scale was playing out as expected. The firm has expanded outside of its initial industries to include affordable housing and credit, and now manages more than $11.5 billion across 40+ companies. These companies have served 13+ million patients and 9+ million students, with impact metrics further defining how and how much impact they created for these individuals. An important part of Marty's success is his belief that private capital can drive innovation, growth, and opportunity for a more equitable society.

From Investment Banking to Impact Venture Capital: Victor Hu

Victor Hu is widely known for cofounding an industry group at Goldman Sachs focused on education technology companies. Coming from a family of pioneers in the education sector—his grandmother was the first female president of a leading teachers' college in Taiwan in the 1960s and helped to educate an entire generation of K-12 school teachers—Victor was very aware of the role education played in the opportunities one had in life. He also grew up in Asia and Africa and witnessed the differences in society when there is a broader commitment to investing in human capital.

Being attuned to this need, Victor began to notice how technology was changing the educational experience while working at Goldman Sachs. This included how we learn and access content for both children and adults, creating opportunities for entrepreneurs to significantly disrupt existing educational institutions. Victor noted this was not just in the

United States but worldwide, from emerging to developed countries. With incumbent businesses struggling to adapt and new businesses in need of capital, it sparked the idea that Goldman Sachs could have a role to play in this transition by advising on strategic decisions and capital raising.

After nearly a decade of building that practice and helping numerous companies navigate these changes, Victor became convinced that there was a way to make money and drive better student outcomes. He could see that education companies informed by experts were designing effective curricula and learning modalities that public schools, higher education institutions, and even corporations found valuable. The number and quality of companies in the human capital market grew so much that Victor believed a growth stage private equity fund could invest in the leaders to amplify their financial and social returns.

Teaming up with James Tieng, another veteran investor in the human capital sector, they formed Lumos Capital Group in 2019 to do just that. As an estimated 23% of jobs globally will need to change in the next five years due to industry transformation, including artificial intelligence, Lumos felt particularly convinced of the need for an impact investor to play a role in helping solve this human capital challenge.[4] Today, Lumos has already invested $150 million in nine companies that empower learners to significantly improve career outcomes and economic mobility.

As these stories illustrate, the path to being an impact investor brings together a person's personal and professional experiences and insights. While many enter the investment industry focused on what sector focus or approach might create the most economic opportunity for themselves, impact investors are not satisfied with that alone. We are critical thinkers who observe market failures, which turn into market opportunities that can create positive outcomes for ourselves and others. The shared belief that the tools of capitalism can create social good *and* wealth, and have been doing it for years, unites our different journeys and skill sets.

Part Two

How to Be an Impact Investor

Chapter Eight

How Impact Can Drive Returns

$\sim$

THE SECURITIES EXCHANGE COMMISSION (SEC) delivers an important warning when it requires the disclaimer that "past performance is not a reliable indicator of future results and investors may not recover the full amount invested."[1] After the longest bull market in U.S. history (from March 2009 to February 2020), when little skill was required to generate gains, the investment industry has been humbled. The extended bull market also meant those managing money today have limited experience in these uncertain market conditions.

A long era of easy money makes experienced, sophisticated investors skeptical of folks who claim they can have their cake and eat it too with impact and financial returns. I am one of those skeptics who is constantly shocked at the investment ideas I hear and read about that have no basis in financial or business theory. When friends ask me for my thoughts on the latest idea they've been pitched, I look to evidence-based research to form an opinion.

Let's return to the financial theory of Harry Markowitz, who famously once said, "Diversification is the only free lunch in investing." In Chapter 5, we learned that Modern Portfolio Theory warns us that limiting an investable opportunity set due to impact can result in lower returns. Yet expertise in the more limited opportunity set that allows for better selection of companies and/or greater value creation during ownership can negate the potential return differential. Those considering impact investments must determine whether the advantages of expertise outweigh the costs of a limited investment universe.

For example, Reach Capital invests in U.S. ventures that provide effective education solutions in early childhood, K-12, higher education, and adult learning. To do this well and to achieve their impact outcomes, they need a whole host of specialty knowledge that is specific to education—from AI and edtech tools to career drivers and culturally relevant curricula. Every partner on their team brings prior experience as an educator, operator, or investor in education, leveraging their expertise to identify companies with real solutions. It's true that Reach's impact lens narrows their investment universe within the education sector, as they will not invest in education companies unlikely to generate impact, but that same lens has driven Reach's strong financial performance.

Academic research also attributes two core factors that drive financial returns for investment portfolios. The first is beta, the systematic risk or volatility compared to the broader market. Having a higher beta signals returns may derive from a heightened correlation to the market, while a low or even negative beta suggests that returns are less related to or negatively correlated to the market's performance. Note that beta can be affected by relative exposure to sectors, geographies, and macroeconomic drivers (e.g. energy prices, inflation, etc.). The second factor is alpha, or an excess return from the investor's skill—which can be related to picking the right companies, sectors, or geographies or to successful market timing.

Impact investing absolutely affects beta and alpha. Many impact investors overweight certain sectors (e.g. healthcare and technology) and underweight other sectors (e.g. energy and industrials) due to the availability of impactful companies in these markets. This results in higher or lower beta than the broader market, which a prospective investor must analyze and consider in portfolio construction. Alpha comes from an investor's skill. The theory that impact expertise improves the ability to select successful companies creates the potential for greater alpha.

Both investment principles point to skill as the key ingredient to impact investing's potential to generate a compelling financial return, despite fewer opportunities for diversification. This is why I insist that being a skilled investor is essential if you intend to be a successful impact investor. What determines skill, and how should you evaluate it?

If we look at investment training programs, from the CFA to an MBA, a high degree of analytical skill is needed to invest. Knowledge of how to analyze financial statements and determine appropriate valuations must be coupled with a strategic understanding of effective business models and the competitive landscape. The ability to evaluate management teams and culture is also essential. Broader perspectives and insights about markets and macroeconomic factors make an investor even more capable of selecting great companies. Discipline, focus, and effective decision-making also make for a great investor. Investing is both science and art.

When evaluating an impact investor's skill, I also look for whether they have a fundamental understanding of how the impact mission might affect, positively or negatively, a business's profitability. Those who refuse to evaluate this potential are leaving financial risks unaddressed. As a staunch advocate for impact investing, I can still acknowledge these common reasons a company striving to drive impact might produce lower financial returns:

- Low price to ensure accessibility
- Limited addressable market
- High costs/low margins to ensure quality
- Managing negative externalities comes at a cost

Conversely, an impact company might produce higher returns on investment based on the following:

- Stronger product-market fit
- Unique distribution channels/deliver models
- Greater insight into policy and demographic changes
- Enhanced branding and customer loyalty
- Better ability to foresee and manage risks
- Lower price sensitivity because of need-based products
- Better attraction and retention of talent
- Ability to unlock nondilutive capital

These lists are only potential effects. The coming chapters will outline practical frameworks for evaluating companies. However, the important takeaway is that there is sufficient basis to believe that impact investing will not inherently perform better or worse. It's all about the skill one has in understanding how the impact is created (e.g. just by lower prices or something innovative that might command a higher price) and how it is managed, both proactively and when times get tough.

Creating and managing a rigorous impact investment process is not easy, but it is rewarding. Investors can enjoy a greater connection to their values and interests when working. Who wouldn't choose to get more than just a financial return from their investment?

Investing is still largely a human capital endeavor, and firms that can attract and retain quality talent have an advantage. Talent pools are essential to successful investments as it is people who conceive ideas, execute diligence and negotiations, and make decisions. Leading investment firms compete for the best talent, knowing how instrumental it is to financial performance. In the case of impact investing, the growth and increasing sophistication of the pool of impact capital is immense.

Trained and dedicated human capital may be the most compelling reason for why impact investing can generate competitive risk-adjusted returns. As an impact investor in residence and adjunct assistant professor at the University of Chicago Booth School of Business since 2017, I've seen firsthand how the next generation of business leaders wants to earn their riches while also doing good. The culture when I was a student at Chicago Booth from 2006 to 2009 was quite different. I never vocalized my interest or intent in anything related to social good, fearing that it would undermine my credibility with my peers. This is the school most known for Milton Friedman's doctrine that the only social responsibility of a business is to maximize shareholder profits. Instead of sharing my curiosity about impact, I kept my head down and focused on acquiring the financial knowledge I went to business school to learn. What happened over the eight years after graduation that convinced the institution it needed an impact investor in residence and a course on impact investing?

Business schools have many stakeholders, but their primary customers are the students. Business school students are perhaps more financially oriented than other graduate school students. Still, many of the Millennials and Generation Z enrolled in MBA programs today think about purpose and mission not just as a goal of philanthropy, but as a guide for how they live their lives. This includes how they spend their money, invest, and choose career paths. The professional golden goose is a job that contributes positively to the world, is aligned with their values, and can still compensate them well. This simple logic explains why my courses attract so many talented students at Chicago Booth.

Chicago Booth is not alone in experiencing this trend. The Impact & Sustainable Finance Faculty Consortium is a global community of educators in the Impact Investing and

Sustainable Finance fields. Today, there are 400+ members from 220+ universities across 40+ countries, including Harvard, Wharton, INSEAD, and many other prestigious institutions.[2] We have come a long way since I had to develop my own syllabus for learning to be an impact investor—from what makes for a good impact investment to how to manage the impact, etc. I applied what I learned, experimented with my personal investments, and used problem-solving skills to create frameworks and tools. Just imagine what these undergrad and MBA students will be able to do with today's more developed academic foundation and formal training from the start of their careers!

We are already seeing the fruits of this training in the quality of talent in the impact investing field. Impact Capital Managers, a trade association of market-rate impact funds in venture capital, private equity, real estate, and private credit, began with 25 funds in 2018 with $5 billion assets under management (AUM) collectively.[3] Today, this network includes more than 100 funds and $80 billion of AUM in its membership base. Leaders of these funds hail from world-class educational institutions and esteemed financial training grounds like Goldman Sachs and Blackstone.

This groundswell in talent mirrors the shift in talent from long-only active management to hedge funds in the early 2000s. The potential to earn more, but from a more intellectually fulfilling way of investing, motivated the talent migration.

Ultimately, having more and better-trained professionals will generate the returns that will drive the future of impact investing. There will be winners and losers, as there are in every asset class and investment strategy. Developing the skills of an impact investor are essential to delivering both financial returns and impact. The following chapters aim to provide a roadmap for skill development.

Chapter Nine

Where Do You Start? Deciding Where Impact Belongs in Your Portfolio

LOOKING AT THE S&P 500 or largest publicly traded companies, it's hard to identify many companies that would immediately strike you as impactful. Sure, Tesla made electric vehicles commonplace, but Elon Musk himself called environmental, social, and governance (ESG) a scam after being dropped from the bellwether index.[1] Other names that might conjure images of do-gooder capitalism include Abbott Labs for creating drugs that save lives or Apple for enabling easier and more ubiquitous communication, both of which we know have much more complicated stories than that.

But let's be serious—if *these* are the best examples we have for impact investing, the industry wouldn't be $1 trillion, and no one would be interested in this book.

There are more examples of impactful private companies. Why? While there is a long history of entrepreneurs building intentionally impactful companies, the support of impact investors in the past decade has created a deeper pipeline of these companies. This, of course, is also supported by consumers desiring healthier and eco-friendly products and younger generations preferring companies aligned with their values. As impact startups become successful, many will go public, thus improving the opportunity set for impact-oriented stock pickers. Take Coursera, a company founded in 2012 to make courses from prestigious universities accessible to more learners, which went public in 2021.

It's also true that public companies often have more complex business models that include many different products, services, or business lines. For example, Unilever is the parent company for Ben & Jerry's and Seventh Generation, but concerns about human rights for workers in plantations that serviced its tea division, including Lipton and PG Tips, led to Unilever's difficulty in selling this business in 2021.[2] While Unilever isn't a perfect company, there is an opportunity for actively engaged investors in its stock to help Unilever create more positive than negative impacts.

The good news is that companies, private or public, that solve societal needs can become very successful and make for a great investment. We have many examples of this going back further than the impact label or the existence of the impact investing industry.

Seventh Generation, owned by Unilever today, is a good example. Alan Newman started the company in 1988 when he bought and rebranded a mail-order catalog focused on energy- and water-saving products.[3] Jeffrey Hollender joined shortly thereafter and continued to deepen its product line of environmentally friendly and nontoxic household cleaning products. They were innovators in the space and likely didn't have a long line of customers looking for such items. Consider some of these field-leading milestones[4]:

- First homecare company to sell unbleached, 100% recycled paper products
- Key lobbyist for the removal of phosphates from dish products and chemical safety testing in homecare products
- First homecare company to disclose ingredients on labels

- 97% of product packaging considered zero waste
- Policy advocate for menstrual equity

The company's front-runner status failed to generate interest from private market investors, and Hollender resorted to taking the company public in 1993 with only $7 million in revenue and –$2.4 million in losses.[5] Not surprisingly, the public listing didn't last long as the company's stage was not well suited for the public market. Hollender took the company private in 1999, bootstrapping his way until sales hit $25 million in 2004. His first venture capital raise wasn't until 2007 (nearly 20 years after the company was founded!) when Renewal Funds, a Canadian impact VC fund, backed Seventh Generation at a $100 million valuation. That capital fueled the company's growth, which was now buoyed by a massive shift in consumer preferences toward eco-friendly products. Generation Investment Management, another impact-oriented investment firm, financed a growth round and finally sold the company to Unilever in 2016 for $700 million.

Today, the company continues to be a leader, profitably prioritizing its impact on the planet and human health. I would argue that Seventh Generation deserves credit for launching today's $101.54 billion-dollar industry of eco-friendly household cleaning products.[6] The company's impact extends well beyond the properties of their products and is a remarkable example of serving unmet needs—capitalism at its best.

A trained impact investor can find these types of opportunities across all asset classes, from pre-seed start-ups to distressed public companies. Real estate owners, private credit lenders, and hedge funds can also invest with an impact strategy. In the next few chapters, we'll walk through the tools to do this successfully. Some tools are more effective with certain stages of companies or certain security types, but we will try to identify the nuances of where/when they are best applied.

Some of these strategies are possible only with a certain amount of capital, sometimes $100,000 (e.g. angel investing) and other times $100,000,000 (e.g. taking a majority stake in a large private company). For all investors, it's essential to have a well-diversified portfolio of investments and to avoid putting all your eggs in one investment. Therefore, you likely need a few million dollars of investable assets before investing directly into impact companies. In most cases, you will be more successful finding impact funds who have the scale necessary to get the job done.

Before diving in, let's cover a few basics so we know how to include impact investing in your portfolio. The first question is always, what is your return objective? As discussed in Chapter 8, expecting your impact investment portfolio to generate similar risk-adjusted returns as a traditional, nonimpact oriented investment is perfectly reasonable. Proper diligence, price discipline, and successful execution are essential to this outcome, and we'll cover the nuances of how impact affects these investment processes in subsequent chapters. Of course, negative financial outcomes may occur, but if that happens, it's important to separate how much of that comes from the impact versus poor skill or bad luck.

When a lower return is realized due to impact, a smart investor will also ask if that was intentional. Accepting less financial gain if you believe it will result in greater impact is also perfectly reasonable. This is very different from a lower return with no extra impact, which I simply call bad investing. Again, the following chapters will help you identify good from bad.

The type of impact and for whom you are creating impact may influence both the return potential and the type of investment. Your returns might be limited if you invest in an area with a smaller addressable market (like improving the livelihood of the formerly incarcerated). However, you can expand the aperture of investment opportunities by pursuing educational or job creation companies that also service the formerly incarcerated. The type of securities may also be a factor; for example, this thesis may lead to a focus on loans to small businesses/sole proprietors that employ the formerly incarcerated. To take a very different angle, if your goal is reducing greenhouse gases, you have the entire industrial, real estate, energy, and utility sectors in your investment universe. Your investment universe could also include all the consumer packaged goods companies needing to reduce their carbon footprints. There is enormous demand coming from these needs, and it most likely creates considerable financial gains for those who have solutions.

Knowing that there is a range of potential financial returns, investors must also start to consider their preferences and constraints regarding time horizon, liquidity, taxes, geography, etc. If you're scratching your head because this sounds like what investors should do anyway, you are right. Impact investing is about good investing just with one more dimension—an impact goal—to what is already not a simple returns-maximizing exercise.

Some investors go through this exercise and decide that 100% of their portfolio should at least strive for impact. As featured in Chapter 7, this is the approach at which Jessica Droste arrived. It required her to focus on optimizing impact and returns versus narrowing in on a single impact theme. Meeting your impact and return objectives requires realistic acknowledgment of the opportunity set.

Other investors decide that a smaller allocation impact (e.g. 5% or 25%) better suits their portfolio. Sometimes this is because of fears of a lower return or a desire to "try out impact" first. In other cases, an investor's specific impact goal may center around a problem without as many commercial solutions or exit opportunities. For example, many family offices want to focus on their local geography, which inherently limits the investment universe. Some examples include enhancing public infrastructure in rural areas or quality jobs in low-income, urban communities. Both examples highlight that a more specific impact objective may also dictate which part of the portfolio the allocation comes from, say real assets/ infrastructure or small business loans (private debt). Again, return expectations for impact real assets may be the same as any other real asset investment, or lower if these intentionally focus on development projects with higher risks.

Some investors make these allocation decisions easily. Others feel more comfortable considering multiple perspectives before they invest. Exploring these questions with your financial advisor makes sense in the latter case. Endowments, pensions, foundations, and family offices often require trustees and professional investors to form a committee to weigh the dimensions and draft an impact policy. This policy often resembles an investment policy statement or can be integrated within one to guide the organization's investment decisions.

Now that we've figured out *where* to make your impact investments, let's put on the hat of the professional investor with many tools at our disposal. Another way to look at the coming chapters is, "This is what I want to see when looking for impact funds and companies." In other words, we'll consider *how* to go about investing in impact.

Chapter Ten

Beyond the Label: Identifying Impactful Companies

<hr />

W HAT MAKES A COMPANY likely to generate a positive impact? The label of an "impact" or "mission-driven" company is insufficient as the industry lacks an accepted standard for what qualifies a company to use such labels. Although a key ingredient, a founder or chief executive officer's (CEO's) desire to be impactful also may not yield the intended result. They must also create a business model conducive to driving impact. Before you sign up to hear from entrepreneurs pitching their purpose-built companies, let's learn tools to help discern the actual versus aspirational impactful companies.

The 5P Framework

Brian Trelstad, a partner at Bridges Fund Management and former chief investment officer at Acumen, created the first tool.[1] His framework helped our team at Impact Engine evaluate our early investments, and it eventually informed our investment criteria. The "5P framework," as we call it at Impact Engine, is a tool to quickly identify the lever within a business that will generate impact. It is not an impact evaluation tool but rather a "cheat sheet" to enable quick identification of the impact model. Here is more about each of the 5Ps.

People

Businesses founded by and/or creating opportunity for people historically underserved by existing markets can be categorized as having people-based impact. The potential to create income through jobs, business ownership, and services that increase the likelihood of gainful employment can create lasting change for individuals and their communities. This strategy can be applied to any industry and asset class. One people-based impact strategy within the financial services sector considers the ownership and management of investment funds. Specifically, some impact investors subscribe to the theory that women and minority fund managers are more likely to invest in women and minority CEOs, which creates a multiplier effect of a single fund investment.

Place

Companies with operations based in locations with limited employment opportunities or upward mobility options can drive economic development and positive impact at the place level. Examples include developing markets and Opportunity Zones in the United States. Given the vast population in these markets and the potential to meaningfully change employment levels, median incomes, and standards of living, the potential scope of place-based impact attracts mission-driven investors. However, companies and investors often encounter hurdles due to these communities' systemic challenges. For example, the need for high levels of job training and robust infrastructure in under-resourced areas may cause operational friction. To help address these challenges, cross-sector partnerships with government agencies and nonprofits may be necessary components of an investment strategy.

Product

Product-level impact involves companies offering products and services that directly create positive impact benefits from a reinforcing tie between revenues and social good. Examples include companies providing access to energy-efficient products, healthcare services, and educational content that drives better outcomes for students. Since customers purchase the company's product based on its efficacy, management teams are incentivized to continuously strengthen and demonstrate the impact of their products. Therefore, impact cannot be easily decoupled from the product if the company is acquired. Focusing on product-based impact limits the investment universe since not all industries offer goods and services that contribute positively to society. Impact investors need to consider the implications of sector concentration and identify other diversification methods within or outside their impact investing portfolio.

Process

Impact at the process level refers to a company's management practices. This may include operational processes, employee wellness, manufacturing, and/or supply chains. All for-profit businesses, regardless of sector or product offering, can optimize management practices. However, generating a lasting social return typically requires the active involvement of the board of directors, a control investment, or other ways of directly influencing strategic decisions. Given this high hurdle for efficacy, investors who want to drive impact at the process level need to think critically about the likely outcome.

Paradigm

A paradigm is a model or pattern of doing business, and investment strategies looking to disrupt existing paradigms and create change at the systems level can be a powerful driver of innovation and impact. Paradigm-based investing strategies might be based upon shifting ownership structures to enable greater wealth creation (e.g. through employee stock ownership plans) or intentionally seek to invest in companies disrupting existing industries in a way that allows greater access/participation (e.g. massively open online courses).

Developing a Theory of Change

All 5Ps are valid strategies for generating positive impact, although each has pros and cons. Once an investor has identified the impact model, deeper research and comprehensive diligence will form their theory of change or impact thesis, reflecting a more thorough framework for evaluating impact.

A theory of change lays out the anticipated causal relation-ship between a company's activities and the changes in society it aims to facilitate. More specifically, it explains why your product offering, if adopted by your target users, will lead to outcomes that ultimately improve society. LuminAID, which won the University of Chicago Booth School of Business's Social New Venture Challenge in 2012, provides a great example. The company manufactures inflatable, floatable, compact, lightweight, solar-powered portable lights for disaster relief/refugee camps. Their theory of change is as follows: "LuminAID's low-cost, low-weight, and compact design will increase light distribution to refugee camps and disaster relief settings. Access to light will enhance safety, facilitate children's learning, and improve the well-being of users."[2] This brief statement effectively summarizes the company's impact thesis.

An impact investor must evaluate a company's theory of change beyond face value and investigate to verify its accuracy. In other words, the due diligence process for an impact investor must explore the evidence for this theory. Let's look at a more complex diligence process from an impact perspective. An investor comes across a company that provides sustainable packaging products. A developing theory of change might be that if the company's customers use this packaging for their products, there will thus be less waste in landfills, improving the planet's health. Questions to ask should include the following:

- What are the materials and properties of the company's packaging products that make it sustainable? How does the company define "sustainability"? Will the product biodegrade in a modern landfill or need to be recycled or composted? What if the packaging ends up in a river; will it decompose? In other words, you must consider potential subsequent or complementary activities the user must do for the theory of the effectiveness of the product to be true.

- How environmentally responsible is the manufacturing process of the sustainable packaging product? Does it require more/less energy, water, etc. than a conventional product like plastic or cardboard? Is the energy source renewable? What are the environmental impacts of the material itself (remember, "not plastic" could be virgin paper products or something that is less consequential and perhaps less resource-intensive to grow)? In this case, technical diligence might be necessary.

- What types of products can utilize the company's packaging? Is the product set a significant contributor to the challenge of waste? For example, if the product is usable only for shoeboxes (because of size, weight, material, etc.), are shoeboxes a significant enough contributor to claim the product reduces waste?

These questions are only the tip of the iceberg. For an impact investor to mitigate climate change, these questions may get them 90% of the way there. However, it would be short-sighted to not also explore impacts on other stakeholders. Employee health safety, for example, is often an important question for any manufacturing company.

Perhaps most important is the diligence of whether the product is compelling enough to replace a conventional product. Think about the shoebox packaging example. One might question whether shoes even need to come in boxes or if there is an easier solution! Other considerations include whether a product can be manufactured at low enough cost to achieve price parity. If not, the company isn't likely to meaningfully compete and will have fairly minimal impact.

Since solving social issues will likely require the efforts of many companies, the role of due diligence centers around verifying a particular company's integral role in the solution. For example, an ACT prep program for disadvantaged teens might improve their odds of getting into college; but, if your impact goal is to improve economic mobility, other efforts will be needed to ensure that they succeed in college and get a quality job. Your evaluation of the company will need to assess the contribution value of the prep program to determine if it's a sufficiently impactful factor.

A theory of change requires some assumptions where there is inconclusive evidence about the ability to drive the desired impact outcomes. Sticking with the previous example, you might assume the importance of ACT scores in college admissions while knowing there are multiple other factors. An impact investor will be intellectually honest about this and acknowledge factors that are not fully known or researchable.

Every investor should appreciate that looking at an investment with an impact lens makes you a better investor. Examining a product's effectiveness, demand drivers, product-market fit, and competitive dynamics from an impact angle lead to better investment decisions. Can you imagine a nonimpact investor looking at this company and not having a clue about what makes a product sustainable or whether replacing conventional packaging is a strategic priority for large consumer packaged goods companies? An impact investor with a network of chief sustainability officers at the largest consumer companies will have an edge in information and the speed in acquiring that information.

In subsequent chapters, I will expand on some additional benefits of developing a strong, well-researched theory of change, including the following:

- It helps avoid "impact washing," or the practice of falsely claiming or embellishing the impact of a company or product (Chapter 11).
- It provides the information needed to conduct measure impact (Chapter 11).
- It develops a blueprint for the investor to know what to prioritize and manage for impact to be enduring as the company grows in size and complexity (Chapters 12 and 13).

Chapter Eleven

If You Don't Measure It, Is It Real?

〜

Some view measurement as an investor's most important action. This is logical, because how can one judge the impact of an investment without evidence? While true, it's also very difficult to measure effectively and very easy to manipulate metrics to mislead or embellish, a practice known as *impact washing*. I've encountered many asset managers launching new impact funds with sensationalized and meaningless metrics like "a billion lives touched." What does "lives touched" even mean? The pictures of seemingly impoverished people of color that the impact fund has "saved" accompany these taglines. No wonder there are impact skeptics.

The good news is that it is possible to measure impact effectively. The bad news is that it's costly, may require many years to provide conclusive evidence, and is often too administratively burdensome, especially for smaller and younger companies with fewer resources. To put it in perspective, the average cost of Phase 1 of a randomized controlled trial for a new pharmaceutical is $4 million, and the average size of a seed round of financing is $3 million. Yes, medical trials for therapeutic drugs are at the extreme end of technical and regulatory requirements. Still, any attempt at doing things in a scientifically credible manner comes at a price. Moreover, the long-term outcomes and impact that a theory of change may hypothesize often takes years to play out.

Developing a Logic Model

Given the challenges, what should a serious impact investor do about measurement? The first step is to do the proper work before making an investment decision, including a well-researched theory of change. With that starting point, an investor can then develop a logic model to determine what should be measured. A logic model is similar to a theory of change, except it is represented in a more chronological manner that details the steps needed to create impact.

1. **Inputs:** What resources do you need to create the desired impact? These can include capital, labor, intellectual property, real assets, inventory, etc.
2. **Activities:** What are the key activities that will drive your impact? This specifies how the input resources will be organized, utilized, etc. For example, capital and talent can be used to manufacture impactful products.
3. **Outputs:** What are the tangible products from the activities? For a cardiovascular healthcare company, for example, this might include the number of patients served and/or the average price they paid.
4. **Impact:** What changes with a causal relationship are identified as a result of the activity over time? Sticking with the cardiovascular healthcare example, an outcome would take an output a step further to the improvement in blood pressure or cholesterol. While such information would be more meaningful, this is where the practical aspect of measurement starts to break down as it would require a significant clinical study to isolate the company's activities to the causal relationship for a health improvement. What if improvements stemmed from changes in exercise and nutrition?
5. **Outcomes:** What key changes are correlated to but not necessarily caused by the activity? This is the most long-term of big-picture goals and in our example might be "decrease in mortality rates of heart

disease patients." It informs the impact, or in other words, is the ultimate purpose of the impact. Yet it is nearly impossible for an investor to measure this long-term outcome.

A sophisticated investor creates a logic model not with the naivete that their investment will be *the* sole contributor to create a desired outcome, but with the humility to know the role a company's activities play in solving complex social issues. No single company will solve climate change or disparities in health outcomes by race or income, but there are still many companies contributing positively to these challenges.

To make these determinations and to create a useful logic model, it's important to understand that impact is the difference in the status of the problem your venture addresses compared to what it would have been without your venture. This requires a counterfactual or an example of what has not happened or would have been the case if the venture's activities did not occur. The most natural counterfactual is what happens with a similar population not "treated" with your program/venture. Yet "similar" can be hard to define. And finding evidence of causal relationships is even more difficult to determine.

These challenges are why outputs, which themselves are not "impact," can provide reasonable believability in the logic model's impact. In other words, if you see evidence of the inputs, activities, and outputs, and there is evidence supporting that these outputs are likely to create the intended impact and outcomes, measuring outputs can serve as a useful proxy. Measuring outcomes can be done cost-effectively, and businesses can be held accountable for such metrics.

Developing a Logic Model: Kaizen Health

Kaizen Health is a healthcare logistics company striving to improve community access to healthcare. When Impact Engine conducted due diligence before deciding to invest in 2013, we created the logic model shown in Table 11.1.

As the logic model articulates, the primary business activities of Kaizen include scheduling and managing transportation for healthcare patients. We didn't automatically assume this was an issue worth solving, but our research revealed that transportation is a significant barrier to healthcare access, often leading to missed appointments and delayed care.[1] We also could see the reasons this is a challenge, especially for lower-income patients or those with certain diseases that restricted mobility. It was a difficult issue to address and required significant resources of vehicles, drivers, and a sophisticated software tool to manage bookings, etc. It also required Kaizen to have a reliable process and the technology to relieve the administrative burden from providers and financial burden

Table 11.1 Logic Model

	Inputs	Activities	Outputs	Impact	Outcomes
Definition	Resources invested in the activity	Concrete actions of the investee	Tangible products from the activity	Changes resulting from the activity, with a causal relationship identified; can be immediate or long-term	Changes correlated with the activity, but not necessarily with a causal effect; can be immediate or long-term
Example (Kaizen Health)	Money, vehicles, people	Scheduling and managing transportation for patients	Number of patients that obtain transportation through Kaizen; number of appointments attended by Kaizen patients; number of provider-scheduled appointments that utilize Kaizen	Change in number of appointments kept by patients; change in number of appointments kept for providers; cost savings for providers	Improved life span of patients

Source: The Impact Engine.

from the patient so they can both focus on the healing and treatment plan.

If Kaizen is successful, the long-term outcome is improved patient lifespans. Although Kaizen is not the only potential provider of such an outcome, stepping back we can see that their impact in increasing appointment attendance is likely to contribute to better health. This impact in turn improves lifespan. This illustrates how identified outputs are closely tied to the likely impacts and can be measured more quickly and cost-effectively than measurable impact.

Kaizen provides a nice case study of how an impact investor can dissect a business's involvement through a logic model. While it is a worthwhile endeavor for a professional impact investor, I have a more simple framework that can lead to similar insights and clues about what to measure.

The Impact Management Project

An industry collaboration that included standard setters (e.g. GIIN, SASB, and UN PRI), as well as practitioners (e.g. companies and impact funds), formed the Impact Management Project (IMP) in 2016 to build consensus on how to measure, manage, and report impact.[2] Together, they determined that the impacts of businesses on people and the planet can be understood across five dimensions (Figure 11.1).

Figure 11.1   Understanding impacts

The IMP reached global consensus that impact can be deconstructed into five dimensions: What, Who, How Much, Contribution and Risk

IMPACT DIMENSION	IMPACT QUESTIONS EACH DIMENSION SEEKS TO ANSWER
□ **WHAT**	• What outcome occurs in period? • How important is the outcome to the people (or planet) experiencing it?
○ **WHO**	• Who experiences the outcome? • How underserved are the affected stakeholders in relation to the outcome?
☰ **HOW MUCH**	• How much of the outcome occurs - across scale, depth and duration?
+ **CONTRIBUTION**	• What is the enterprise's contribution to the outcome, accounting for what would have happened anyway?
△ **RISK**	• What is the risk to people and planet that impact does not occur as expected?

Source: The Impact Management Project. (n.d.). https://impactfrontiers.org/norms/five-dimensions-of-impact/

The model breaks down each of the five dimensions into a question-based approach to assess the potential impact and impact risks of a company or project. Similar to the logic model, these prompts help evaluate cause and effect, necessary inputs, and the potential magnitude of impact that will inform what you should measure.

How to Evaluate Impact Metrics

With a solid understanding of the theory of change and how to implement potential metrics, let's talk about how to measure the output metrics. Yes, this is not just a theoretical exercise—investors need to be able to provide meaningful data to the identified metrics. Now is when you should start to wonder if "lives touched" is a usable metric!

Impact investing practitioners without the budget and time horizon of randomized control trials often utilize key performance indicators (KPIs) as key data sources. These practical indicators can be measured by the company cost effectively and regularly from their own business operations. We'll explore examples here, but there are three key elements when determining an effective KPI for impact investments.

- It has to connect to a theory of change. Yep, no escaping the theory of change! Connecting to the theory will guide you to the appropriate KPIs (hint: look at outputs).
- It must be practical to collect. Will you obtain this data through customer surveys or point-of-sale information? How much will your collection mechanism cost, and would it protect the appropriate privacy of customers?

- KPIs must be significant enough to warrant the collection effort. Data substantiating whether your customers are downloading your edtech app, for example, is not as important as how often they utilize the edtech app.

With these principles in place, there are a variety of quantitative and qualitative collection methods to consider.

- Interviews
- Focus groups
- Rubrics
- Surveys
- Observations
- Company systems
- Most significant change

Each method can be practical and useful and connect to your theory of change but requires thoughtful analysis to determine what will be most effective. I've found that investors of every asset class and stage have viable options if they consider measurement under these circumstances and do not expect a perfectly controlled scientific approach.

While more time efficient and cost-effective, using KPIs is not easy. It does cost something extra, even if just in terms of the time and attention it takes an investor to evaluate these factors. However, for me, and any authentic impact investor, our desire to fundamentally enhance our understanding of impact and ensure that it's worth all the effort and attention warrants the investment in metrics. Impact is why I am an investor, so of course, I want to understand it.

How Impact Metrics Can Help the Traditional Investor

Not all investors are driven primarily by impact, and some may question the value of the effort required to be impactful. Some asset managers measure and manage impact only because clients require it. However, I contend that information from impact diligence and management can improve traditional investors' outcomes. How? Taking a step back, all investors—impact and otherwise—really have only three jobs: analyze, decide, and manage/react. Rinse and repeat. With more information and better analysis, I believe that investors, regardless of mission, can better allocate resources to companies that create optimal social (and economic) value. Capital resources should flow to effective allocators who choose and manage their investments effectively for shareholders and society. Therefore, *all investors*, not just impact investors, should dedicate resources to and utilize impact measurement.

So the question is: what purpose do KPIs serve? A company may utilize KPIs to guide management decisions or to assist in a fundraise. An investor might implement them to determine where to allocate resources or capital or to illustrate impact beyond a multiple on invested capital (MOIC). Some might even use KPIs to support the unlikely idea that a company can affect public policy. These each represent legitimate reasons to measure outcomes. All also support why I believe impact measurement is worthwhile for *all* investors and shouldn't be a penalty or cost burden only for impact investors. Companies should share the load as we know it all has an impact regardless of whether it is measured. Regardless of who assumes the cost, the real work of impact management only begins with measurement.

Building Better Businesses: Impact Management

~

Theoretically, if an investment is in an impact fund's portfolio, they've decided it's impactful, right? That's only the beginning of the story. The investor's role doesn't stop with the initial impact determination. What happens over the course of subsequent years will make the company more or less impactful than the initial assessment. Day-to-day decisions, such as how to manage through a difficult year, as well as big decisions, such as selling to a competitor, can have a very big effect.

An investor's involvement with the company can significantly influence these decisions. For example, the governance rights of board directors carry a vote in the decision of a potential sale. Company executives often seek investors' feedback and insight about decisions and impact implications of new product launches or of serving a particular customer segment.

An impact investor has many tools to influence impact, and I've categorized them into three approaches: communication and engagement, terms and incentives, and legal structures. Some tools mirror those of a traditional investor seeking to create value (e.g. helping a company raise capital). However, an impact investor has different goals, takes a unique approach, and utilizes novel tools, such as impact incentives, to manage impact management.

Let's dive in.

Communication and Engagement

It's powerful for investors to speak about their impact objectives in their first conversation with a chief executive officer (CEO) or potential investee. In an era of abundant potential sources of capital, especially as the venture capital and private equity industries have grown tremendously, embracing impact allows investors to differentiate themselves. Like most human interactions, entrepreneurs are looking for signs of trustworthiness. What better way than to be transparent about what you stand for and why you would invest?

Focusing on impact allows an investor to build a deeper relationship that could be valuable in a competitive financing round. Impact Engine has participated in many competitive financing rounds where our participation was prioritized despite writing the smallest check. Why? The round was oversubscribed, but the entrepreneur wanted at least one investor who was fully aligned with their goals for the company and could both understand and advocate for certain choices down the road because of our alignment and expertise. We earned a place in these situations because of our impact orientation.

Being clear about your goals and addressing concerns about impact during the due diligence process also sets the tone to enable engagement post-close. When you conduct diligence and ask the type of questions posed in Chapter 10, it will make sense to the management company why you're following up on these same questions later as the business evolves.

Kaizen Health, for example, had an opportunity to expand its business in 2021 into transportation for K-12 school students. This might seem like a distraction *or* a huge opportunity to a nonimpact investor. They might ask, "What will it require in terms of investment in resources, what is the potential market opportunity, what are the margins, and how does it change the long-term valuation and exit potential?" As an impact investor, we asked the same questions but also wanted to understand the potential impact. It did not surprise Kaizen when we had these questions, as we were up front about our goals and aligned with the CEO, Mindy Knebel, from the beginning. It allowed us to partner with Mindy to help determine if this was an attractive growth opportunity that would serve her financial and impact goals.

If we go back to Kaizen's logic model in Chapter 11, transporting students does not fit within this framework. However, that does not mean it would not be impactful. We learned that the business opportunity came from a large public school district, seeking a solution for both special needs students and refugee families. Their transportation needs were complex and poorly served by the existing school bus system. While the output, impact, and outcomes differed from a transportation business focused on improving access to healthcare, the inputs and activities did not require much change in Kaizen's operations. Expanding the business would allow Kaizen to drive more impact in the form of access to education, while not risking their impact in improving access to medical care.

Beyond crossroads like those Kaizen faced, investors build a strong reputation by adding value. Common value creation opportunities include capital raising, customer introductions, talent acquisition, and mergers and acquisition (M&A). Although impact investors have an area of expertise, often falling into one of these categories, our toolkit brings additional benefits.

Impact investors bring a broader pool of potential capital sources to support a company's financing than traditional financing, including public and philanthropic sources. DBL Partners provided critical assistance to ZOLA Electric, a company that provides affordable, reliable, and renewable energy to communities in Africa that lack access to electricity.[1] DBL helped the company raise $45 million to finance the leasing of its systems in Tanzania, in part through a $5 million grant from USAID's Development Innovation Ventures program, along with low-interest loans from several private mission-driven investors, including the David and Lucile Packard Foundation, Ceniarth, and the Calvert Foundation.

Impact investors also help companies create and implement revenue growth strategies. Bridges U.S. Sustainable Growth Fund, an impact private equity fund, helped Springboard Education identify a federal voucher program that could provide a new source of revenues for the high-quality after-school education company.[2] Bridges' market expertise and focus on social impact factored significantly in the discovery of the federal program. Bridges then worked with company management to develop operational capabilities, including marketing, enrollment, and reimbursement, to qualify for and successfully tap into the voucher program.

Terms and Incentives

Investors may support value creation informally through discussions or other engagement, but often, and especially in cases where an investor owns a significant stake in the company, formally. There are three broad categories of terms that impact investors can utilize to create impact.

> *Commitment statements* are written agreements to manage a business with the intent to create impact outcomes. This enterprise-level commitment is often engineered into the foundational documents of an operating business. Here is an example in a Delaware LLC provided by RPCK Rastegar Panchal LLP (RPCK), a law firm with a long history of serving impact-driven companies and investors:
>
> The purpose of the Company shall include creating a material positive impact on society and the environment, taken as a whole, from the business and operations of the Company.

a. In discharging the duties of their positions and in considering the best interests of the Company, a [manager] [managing member] shall consider the effects of any action or inaction on:

  i. the members of the Company;

  ii. the employees and work force of the Company, its subsidiaries, and its suppliers;

  iii. the interests of its customers as beneficiaries of the purpose of the Company to have a material positive impact on society and the environment;

  iv. community and societal factors, including those of each community in which offices or facilities of the Company, its subsidiaries, or its suppliers are located;

  v. the local and global environment;

  vi. the short-term and long-term interests of the Company, including benefits that may accrue to the Company from its long-term plans and the possibility that these interests may be best served by the continued independence of the Company; and

vii. the ability of the Company to create a material positive impact on society and the environment, taken as a whole.

In this case, an investor could require a company to amend their formation documents if such a commitment did not already exist. Alternatively, an investor could require a written commitment by the company to use the financing proceeds directly to advance a stated impact outcome or project, such as the following:

- Green retrofitting of a facility
- Providing health benefits to employees
- Expanding the company's product or services offerings to a new frontier market where it can improve lives or the environment
- Complying with an ESG action plan developed with investors to help address identified ESG shortcomings

In some cases, investors can negotiate remedies for a company's failure to comply with mission-related use of proceeds requirements, such as redemption rights. However, in most cases that may disrupt the deal dynamics, especially if multiple investors are around the table. Impact investors need to find ways to enforce impact without it becoming an additional legal or administrative burden.

Disclosure requirements obligate companies to report impact KPIs, ESG metrics, DEI stats, etc. These are tailored to align interests and reinforce accountability among the parties. Here is one example, again from a legal agreement written by RPCK:

"Within thirty (30) days following the end of each calendar quarter, the Company shall provide to the Investor a written report of certain financial and impact metrics to be determined by the Investor including, without limitation, gross revenue, leverage, number of jobs created, amount of carbon reduction, number of sustainable livelihoods improved, and disaggregated employee, management and Board data by gender."

Incentives are when explicit benefits are tied to impact goals, ranging from impact KPIs to ESG and DEI metrics. These are designed to align the financial incentives of the management team with the impact goals of the fund or enterprise. Examples include the following:

- Management stock grants with vesting tied to impact targets
- Discount on a convertible note based on achieving impact goals
- Price ratchets down if impact KPIs are not achieved

Marty Nesbitt's firm, The Vistria Group, effectively uses its influence as a control investor in private middle market companies. The firm not only has a board seat but typically controls the board with a majority of the seats filled by its team members or selected representatives. This allows The Vistria Group to control the budget, decide on mergers and acquisitions, and even set incentive plans for executives—all with the lens of an impact investor, aiming for both financial and impact success. For example, Marty and his team assess diversity, equity, and inclusion (DEI) for each portfolio company to determine the opportunities they have to increase DEI outcomes. This includes more inclusive hiring practices, as well as retention and promotion rates for underrepresented people. The Vistria Group has also created financial incentives for improvement within its portfolio companies because it believes that diverse teams that are focused on driving quality and outcomes create more equitable performance and a more inclusive workplace.

Recently, there has been a surge of interest in tying specific impact metrics of a fund to the fund manager's compensation. It is still relatively rare due to the complexity, cost, and lack of market standards. It's difficult to decide what specific metrics are the most relevant, let alone what is a realistic threshold for a fund manager to be able to achieve given so many uncontrollable variables. Although it will likely invite some manipulation among fund managers to ensure their own success, I believe this practice will become more common as more data is collected from the impact investing industry.

Legal Structures

There are also opportunities for impact investors to build impact, or impact protection, into the structure of companies.

B Corp Certification is a designation for businesses that meet certain standards of verified performance, accountability, and transparency regarding factors such as employee benefits and charitable giving, supply chain practices, and input materials. It's a rigorous process for a company to become a B Corp but does not change a business's tax status or charter. Instead, it's a way to communicate to stakeholders—customers, community, employees, etc.—that the company is committed to impact. There are more than 8,000 B Corps today, including well-known brands like TOMS, Allbirds, and Warby Parker and multinational companies like Danone.[3]

A Public Benefit Corporation (PBC) is required to have at least a stated public benefit in its certificate of incorporation, which is conferred by state law in the United States. This thus requires the company's board of directors to account for the interests of multiple stakeholders when exercising fiduciary duties and making decisions about managing and exiting the business. In contrast, board directors of C corporations, LLCs, or S corporations are accountable only for shareholders' economic value. We structured Impact Engine as a PBC in order to have the full fiduciary right to manage the business to drive impact optimized with financial returns, and our stated public benefit is to grow the impact investing ecosystem. There are 19 publicly traded PBCs today, including Vital Farm and Laureate Education.[4]

Employee stock ownership plans (ESOPs) enable employees to own a company, and perpetual purpose trusts (PPTs) specify a purpose or mission for the company to ensure that leaders focus on mission over profit. Both are exciting and complicated, and we'll cover them in detail in Part Three.

From engagement to structure, what should be clear now is that impact investing is a verb, not a noun. It's something you *do*. It takes effort from day one and every day after that to build an impactful company, and investors have a large role in ensuring this happens. With that effort comes many benefits to the investor and the company. Building an impactful business does not happen overnight and is not guaranteed even for the most well-intentioned entrepreneur. The ups and downs of any successful business require critical analysis, sound decision-making, and focused execution. Doing so to create enduring impact brings a greater sense of purpose that can create a powerful motivating force.

Chapter Thirteen

Stuck in the Mud: When Impact Gets Complicated

~

I want to be honest with you—despite the best intentions and plans, impact does not always translate into a competitive advantage, better margins, new sources of capital or revenues, enhanced brand recognition, or better talent. The same is true for every company, impactful or otherwise. The best plans with the best teams do not always result in success. However, impact investors have a harder job because when a business is going through a rough patch, they have to help management get through it while holding them accountable to the mission. They can't approach layoffs, price increases, chief executive officer (CEO) changes, and other decisions as a simple math equation. Let's look at a few common situations I've observed in the market.

A Business Model Shift and a Leadership Transition: OnlineMedEd

Victor Hu's Lumos Capital Group is an investor in OnlineMedEd (OME), a global medical education platform that helps students master medical knowledge, pass exams, and succeed in residency with easy-to-digest content.[1] The digital curriculum was developed with a proven pedagogical approach by Dr. Dustyn Williams, a recognized teacher-practitioner in medicine. He cofounded the company with Jamie Fitch, a data-driven CEO, trained as a clinical epidemiologist.[2]

OME's impact thesis centered on decreasing health outcome disparities by geography, race, and ethnicity, which unfortunately continue to persist. While the reasons for these outcomes are complex and multifaceted, the lack of diversity in medical practitioners and implicit biases in delivering care to diverse patients is notable. In the United States, 6% of active physicians are Latino, 5% are Black, and 36% are female.[3] By providing a limited free version of OME's curriculum, they believed that the diversity of medical practitioners and the quality of medical practitioners coming from diverse educational backgrounds would improve.

At the time of investment, OME had users in 191 countries and was used by more than 80% of U.S. medical students. Part of the growth strategy when Lumos invested was to expand a business-to-business (B2B) model, selling to medical schools to provide OME's complete curriculum for free to *all* medical students, and not just those with the financial capacity to pay.

Unfortunately, the B2B offering cannibalized the B2C subscriptions more than anticipated, getting in the way of OME achieving its goals and putting investors' capital at risk. As an impact investor, Lumos had to develop a strategy to get the company back on track while maintaining its mission to improve access to medical education to improve healthcare outcomes for more people. This involved some tough decisions, including changes to its subscription pricing and a leadership change to navigate the challenges ahead while staying true to OME's mission. With each decision, Lumos had to consider the impact on multiple stakeholders—most notably medical students and the broader healthcare system, including patients—versus simply maximizing their returns.

I got my bird's-eye view of this transition and transformation since Impact Engine is a co-investor alongside Lumos; and things are on the right track with the new CEO that Victor and his team identified. Their leadership in a complex and high-stakes situation illuminated the analysis and judgment calls that an impact investor makes versus an ordinary investor who might quickly resort to short-term profit-maximizing tactics. It would have been a far easier path to simply discontinue the B2B business, which is likely to create greater accessibility, but Lumos believed that reaching more medical students would create a competitive advantage, enhancing both impact and profitability long-term.

Mergers and Acquisitions: Regroup Therapy

Mergers and acquisitions are common strategies at the growth stage, when a company has reached the limit of organic growth. Impact Engine had to decide whether a merger would maintain, improve, or harm the impact for Regroup Therapy, a telemental health company in which we first invested in 2015.

When founder David Cohn created the company pre-pandemic, telehealth for behavioral health was not as widely adopted despite the clear need, especially for those living in areas of the United States with a limited supply of mental health professionals. When David observed that more than 50% of the counties in the United States don't have a mental health professional, he developed a secure, Health Insurance Portability and Accountability Act (HIPPA)–compliant, virtual care platform for health systems, clinics, corrections facilities, and other institutions in rural areas to offer to their patients. Notably, more than 80% of the patients lived in counties designated as Provider Shortage Areas. This B2B model also enabled insurance coverage in most cases.

After roughly five years of operations and significant growth, Regroup had an opportunity to merge with a competitor. Insight Telepsychiatry operated a similar telepsychiatry business; however, it managed a more concentrated business in emergency situations. For example, these situations might include patients who come to a hospital with a mental health emergency and require psychiatrists to diagnose and treat them effectively. The promise of the combined entities was a larger, more diversified business and the largest staff of psychiatrists in the United States. However, Insight didn't have the same origin story, focus on impact, or patient population as Regroup. Impact Engine's diligence process included conversations with Insight's management team, investors, and board members. Despite the difference in intentionality, we decided that the business was aligned with Regroup and that shareholders and directors around the table would try to grow, rather than dismantle, Regroup's impact business model.

COVID-19 hit the United States less than six months after the companies merged (and rebranded as Array Behavioral Care) and the widespread adoption of therapy sessions from home ensued. Despite the fast growth seen by other telemental health providers, Array's scheduled and emergency services were negatively impacted as the risk of exposure to the virus from a visit to the hospital or clinic drove many patients to defer care. The company had to decide whether to expand into an "at-home" delivery model. This model shift could fuel the growth of the business but would serve a demographic of patients outside of Provider Shortage Areas. The board and management team decided that the benefit of diversification outweighed the risk. The growth of teletherapy at home presented an opportunity to Array without compromising the company's B2B focus that creates accessible and affordable care.

Today, the number of patients served in Provider Shortage Areas continues to grow while Array has also successfully diversified the business. The opportunity to expand proved possible without negatively affecting its ability to serve those with more limited access to care.

Exits: Edovo

Exits are another moment in a company's life cycle that exposes impact risk. Edovo was founded by Brian Hill in 2013 to reduce recidivism rates, or the number of formerly incarcerated who return to prison. Research indicates that access to education leads to 43% lower rates of recidivism and to 8–28% increased odds of obtaining post-release employment.[4] Yet Hill saw firsthand, through personal experiences, how limited access to education was holding inmates back from the necessary economic and social connections and experiences once they left prison. On average, just one in five incarcerated individuals nationally had access to educational programming while the rest were left to daytime television.[5] Edovo introduced the concept of bringing secure wireless networks and tablets into the prison dayrooms to deliver daily access to self-improvement content. Edovo curated a platform that could reach individuals at any learning level, from GED curriculums and vocational training to anger management and parenting courses. Of course, they had to be protected from unintended uses as well as the potential physical damage from falling on concrete floors. The business model relied on correctional facilities using education dollars to pay for the infrastructure and license the software.

Edovo was successful after an initial launch in Philadelphia's prison system and quickly expanded into other cities and states. By 2023, Edovo was available in more than 400 sites, serving nearly 500,000 incarcerated individuals a year with nearly 60 million hours of engagement time on the platform to date.[6] This resulted in more than 4 million education, job training, and social/emotional courses completed annually, including more than 200,000 GED or certification courses.

While the company created tremendous impact, it came through many pivots as correctional institutions proved unwilling to pay for the infrastructure and eventually leaned on entrenched prison phone companies to install the hardware. Through a cycle of buying, growing, and then selling a phone company, Edovo constantly wrestled with the balance of scaling the impact or profitably delivering to a fraction of the market. Despite clear demand from the end user (the incarcerated learner), the correctional facility's demand and willingness to pay never reached a level that would enable education for all but the same small portion of the population it was currently reaching. While the company was able to generate several millions of dollars in annual revenues, and even achieve profitability, its board had a decision to make about the future trade-offs between scaled impact and necessary investment with fairly flat financials.

Edovo had several opportunities to sell to the traditional telecommunications providers or other strategics profitably, but there was significant impact risk as they were not aligned with Edovo's mission. Alternatively, Edovo could have expanded its reach into other industries, but they saw firsthand how companies consistently disinvested in the corrections space leaving poor offerings that did little to support incarcerated learners. Ultimately, the board decided to return capital and convert to a non-profit to keep its impact intact. Looking at the impact, Edovo was a success, and its unprecedented scale has decreased the transaction costs to serve the incarcerated and is now enabling a resurgence of investment. However, its financial return to impact investors, including Impact Engine, was less than we expected as an early-stage venture investment, and it was fundamentally the desire for scaled impact that prevented that financial success.

I share the story of Edovo to remain intellectually honest that impact investing has upsides, limitations, and risks that at times differ from traditional investing. Although the potential to create similar risk-adjusted returns plus significant impact exists, so does risk. You must do your due diligence. If it sounds too good to be true, there is a chance it is too good to be true. But isn't that true of all investing?

Part Three

The Impact
Opportunity Set

Chapter Fourteen

Where Can You Find Impact Investments?

Now that we know what makes a company impactful and how an investor can best manage that potential impact, we're ready to find opportunities. Good ideas can come from anywhere. I recommend analyzing companies you come across as a consumer or normal citizen to become really good at spotting great investments. You don't have to be a professional investor to do this.

The best way to start is to apply the 5P framework, described in Chapter 10, to companies you come across daily, like new food brands at the grocery store or targeted advertisements in your social media feed. Use this framework to determine whether you think impact is possible. Don't limit yourself to things that show up in your workplace inbox or someone pitching you an idea. Pattern recognition only comes with significant repetition. And brilliant ideas of your own, like when you have a lightbulb go off about how a for-profit business model can solve for access to clean water in geographies far from the Great Lakes (the most valuable bodies of water in the world), happen only when you start looking at the world differently. The best investors think about market opportunities 24/7, not just when sitting at their desks.

It's also important to remember that impact investing is relevant and active in most asset classes. A common misconception that impact investing is limited to venture capital stems from the history of impact investing and the association between innovation and social change. However, when reflecting on Part 2 and the various business models for driving impact, it should be possible for companies of all sizes and at all stages of their business life cycle to implement management approaches to benefit employees, reduce the carbon intensity in their supply chain, design new products with impact intentionality, enter new geographies or distribution channels, expand reach, etc.

The Global Impact Investing Network (GIIN) conducts an annual industry survey to provide insights about how the field is evolving. Notably, we can see significant diversification in AUM allocation by business stage (Table 14.1).

It's worth noting that larger companies account for a disproportionate amount of this diversification as they receive more total funding and that this diversification would skew toward seed and venture stage companies if done instead by number of companies.

We also see in GIIN's report that the proportion of impact AUM was well allocated across all major asset classes (Table 14.2).

Investors can provide equity or debt to companies, making private credit a viable asset class for impact investors just as much as private equity. Other asset classes, like real estate, also offer unique opportunities for impact that focus more on accessibility, affordability, quality of life, and sustainability than a business model.

GIIN's report also notes impact investors actively deploy capital to different geographic regions (Table 14.3).

Table 14.1 AUM Allocation by Business Stage

Business Stage	Percentage of AUM
Mature, private companies	34%
Growth stage	30%
Mature, publicly trading companies	27%
Venture stage	7%
Seed/start-up stage	2%

Source: Data from Hand et al., 2023

Table 14.2   Impact AUM Across Asset Classes

Asset Class	Percentage of AUM
Private equity	26%
Private debt	22%
Real assets	17%
Public equity	14%
Public debt	14%
Equity-like debt	2%
Deposits and cash equivalents	1%
Other	1%

Source: Data from Hand et al., 2023

Table 14.3   Capital in Different Geographic Regions

Geographic Region	Percentage of AUM
U.S. & Canada	29%
Western, Northern & Southern Europe	23%
Sub-Saharan Africa	10%
Latin America & Caribbean	8%
South Asia	8%
Eastern Europe, Russia & Central Asia	6%
Southwest Asia	5%
East Asia	5%
Oceania	4%
Middle East & North Africa	3%

Source: Data from Hand et al., 2023

Finally, GIIN dissects the dollars allocated across sectors (Table 14.4).

Table 14.4 Dollars Allocated Across Sectors

Sector	Percentage of AUM
Energy	17%
Financial services (excluding microfinance)	13%
Healthcare	9%
Microfinance	8%
Food and agriculture	7%
Infrastructure	7%
Housing	6%
Information and communication technology	5%
Forestry and timber	5%
Manufacturing	4%
Water and sanitation	2%
Education	2%
Arts and culture	0.1%
Other	14%

Source: Data from Hand et al., 2023

While the possibilities for impact investing are endless, the remaining chapters focus on markets and strategies that present unique opportunities and challenges for corporations to try to solve and impact investors to support.

Three common themes—economic opportunity, environmental sustainability, and health equity—represent sizable markets with key societal challenges that businesses can address. We'll cover these in Chapters 15–17, with a primary focus on private companies that have demonstrated an ability to deliver impact and financial returns, as well as new subthemes and business models worth exploring.

Chapter Fifteen

Economic Opportunity

—— ≈ ——

THE OXFORD ENGLISH DICTIONARY defines the American dream as "the ideal that every citizen of the United States should have an equal opportunity to achieve success and prosperity through hard work, determination, and initiative."[1] It's a worthy ideal for sure, but what makes it possible?

Many point to education, which Horace Mann famously called the "great equalizer of the conditions of men." Yet how can it be an equalizer if access to quality education is unequal and the lack of education or access to poor education can lead to lifelong gaps in employment and earnings?

Poverty and income inequality remain real challenges globally. According to the 2022 U.S. Census, 11.5% of Americans live in poverty.[2] This represents an increase of 4.6% from 2021, the largest one-year increase in history. This equates to 37.9 million Americans who earn less than $13,590 annual income for individuals and $23,030 for a family of three. Moreover, with a real median income of $74,580 in 2022, a 2.3% decline from the prior year, as well as a steady contraction of the middle class over the past five decades from 61% in 1971 to 50% in 2022, the addressable market for solutions to create greater economic mobility is growing exponentially.

Many people say politicians should address this inequality, but I contend that they can't eliminate it alone. As an impact investor looking for societal challenges that need solutions, which I broadly label *economic opportunity*, I am acutely aware of the magnitude of these challenges and know impact investing provides a critical complement to government policies and philanthropic donations. Impact investments also create necessary incentives and support corporations to address and solve market failures.

To identify and invest in solutions to achieve economic security—the ability for individuals or households to meet and maintain their basic needs—impact investors need to have some understanding of the market failures that cause actual or perceived risk of economic insecurity.

As an economics major, I came to believe that the best indicator of economic health in society is whether citizens *feel* secure about their future regardless of socio-economic status. While the wealthy can often create this security by selling assets, certain situations—such as professional athletes having little employment security and not enough savings from a short career, women risking their financial future when leaving an abusive partner, and retired or disabled people coping with the monumental costs of healthcare—underscore why most people need extensive planning to avoid the feeling of economic insecurity.

The government plays a role in mitigating this risk by creating social safety nets. This includes Social Security benefits, Medicare, disability, unemployment benefits, and even incentives like tax deductions for retirement plans that help households build a cushion. The United States is known for having more limited safety nets than Europe, and many credit this philosophy for motivating hard work and entrepreneurship. There is research behind both sides of the argument, and again I'm not here to pick sides. I simply note the market failure, which is that almost 40 million Americans are living in poverty where the safety nets aren't sufficient to achieve economic stability.

As economic insecurity has become an increasingly common problem, it's important to identify the causes. One is the growth in income volatility or the lack of predictable, consistent, and sufficient income. This is not just the inability to be employed or low wages. The lack of reliable benefits, from pensions to affordable health insurance (e.g. for Uber drivers or other gig jobs), also creates economic insecurity.

Technology presents another causal factor that has driven this trend and made it increasingly difficult for policymakers to solve. The speed of innovation requires near-constant acquisition of new skills and renders many jobs obsolete. Globalization is another driver as both manufacturing jobs and white-collar technology jobs have been outsourced overseas. These changes are driven by market forces, a necessary and good thing in a capitalist society. There are positives to these changes; we just need to find ways to help society adapt with abundant opportunities for quality jobs and secure income.

Our labor laws and norms haven't evolved apace with the disruption of technology on the nature of employment across many industries. For example, gig workers who work full-time but on a contract basis do not meet the typical requirement of full-time employment to qualify for benefits. Policymakers are trying to solve for these needs, but legislation often takes a long time, and this time burden exacerbates suffering and loss while laws catch up to society's needs.

For-profit businesses have the potential to create solutions for these needs quickly by making and selling effective products and services. This is not a new concept. The banking industry, with offerings from savings accounts to mortgages, enables households to build financial safety nets and home ownership. The insurance sector helps spread risk so that an individual's loss from a car crash, natural disaster, etc. reduces the risk of catastrophic loss.

However, only some have access to these services, and if they do, the price point might adversely affect their financial situation. According to the FDIC in 2021, 5.9 million or 4.5% of U.S. adults do not have a checking or savings account. Another 14.1% is underbanked, meaning that they have to use alternative services, like money orders or pawn shops, to cash a check or pay bills.[3] This often occurs because of the timing of when wages are paid and when bills are due. Payday loans, and other services, typically impose high fees and interest rates that load consumers with debt that they are unlikely to be able to service, creating a vicious cycle of debt.

Finding the Right Solutions to Create Economic Opportunity

Impact investors with a goal of creating economic opportunity must look for both *effective* and *accessible* solutions. Effective means that there should be a theory of change that the company enables economic stability and mobility, perhaps through increased earnings or decreased debt burden. Accessible means it must be affordable and via a delivery model that reaches many.

Let's go back to the beginning to look for solutions: education. As noted, many believe that education is the basis of economic opportunity as empirical evidence supports that higher average lifetime earnings correlate with higher levels of education attained. According to the National Center for Education Statistics, in 2021, the median earnings of those with a master's or higher degree were $74,600, or 21% higher than the earnings of those with a bachelor's degree ($61,600).[4] Similarly, the median earnings of those with a bachelor's degree were 55% higher than the earnings of those who completed high school ($39,700).

I experienced this firsthand as my immigrant parents personally and financially sacrificed for me to attend prestigious schools and participate in supplementary programs, affording me greater financial mobility. However, not everyone lives in neighborhoods with strong schools or can afford to send their children to a private school or to hire tutors to improve academic performance. Unfortunately, access to quality education in the early years of life snowballs into more or less opportunities to access quality higher education and then eventually quality jobs.

An impact investor with this perspective has many opportunities to drive economic opportunity through education. These opportunities include increasing admissions, affordability, and graduation rates from preschool through adult learning.

For example, Sarah Horn cofounded ReUp Education in 2015 to serve the 40% of students in the United States who start but never finish post-secondary education.[5] Prior to ReUp, she spent 15 years creating, implementing, and managing student retention programs at dozens of colleges and universities across the country. She observed that students leave college not only because they lack academic preparedness. Instead, many leave because colleges were unprepared to personalize learning to meet students' varied academic backgrounds and learning gaps.

Other reasons cause students to leave college, including difficulty balancing personal and professional commitments (particularly those having to work to pay for school), lack of financial resources, and physical and emotional health challenges. While schools put effort into retaining students, once a student drops out, there isn't any real solution to help them return or complete what they started. They leave on the table the potential increase in career earnings through promotion or a career change and their students' sense of accomplishment and worth.

Sarah built ReUp to support re-enrollment students and degree completion by offering personalized support and planning using technology and one-on-one coaches. The company partners with schools and university systems, which, in turn, benefit from re-enrollment through increased tuition revenue and graduation rates. ReUp measures its impact by the percentage of students who persist in college for the first six months through ReUp. This shorter-term metric indicates the likelihood of graduation. As of 2023, the company generated persistence rate of 69% of students with more than 500 ReUp students graduating each year.

Another education solution is BookNook, which focuses on literacy for elementary school students with a stated mission to ensure equitable access to rigorous and personalized instruction through technology innovation. Why? About one in three children struggle with reading at some point in elementary school, and students are four times more likely to go to college if they master reading by the third grade and seven times more likely to complete college if they don't need remedial reading support in high school.[6] The company's proven and effective virtual literacy tutoring platform delivers high-quality instruction via its proprietary software and processes. Students receive content from vetted tutors in real time or synchronously, a term that became much more familiar to students and families in 2020 when the COVID-19 pandemic brought live, virtual learning into students' homes.

BookNook had seven years of operating experience by 2020 and utilized real, live tutors versus games and AI-generated tutoring because the former created more measurable improvements in reading levels. A recent study in Texas also demonstrated that fifth-grade students completing 18+ BookNook sessions moved on average from the 50th to the 75th percentile of student literacy results. Results like these positioned the company to meet the Department of Education's ESSA Tier III standards of evidence. After recently completing a randomized trial, BookNook also met the criteria for Tier I standards (the highest standard of evidence achievable for an educational intervention).

BookNook's impact results, and the company's investment in measuring them, outshines its competitors who utilize technology to maximize margins.

Policymakers and philanthropists also attempt to improve outcomes in college graduation and childhood literacy by funding programs and setting school standards. However, companies motivated by profits—driven by effective services that create a competitive advantage—can meet these needs more quickly and at scale. These market-based solutions also have limited downside, as they don't interfere with and perhaps might even inform policy changes.

Though addressing one market failure will not address all economic instability or immobility, the goal should be to increase the probability of stability for as many as possible. ReUp, BookNook, and other education companies contribute to this goal as does another subsector of economic opportunity: inclusive and effective financial services like banking and housing.

Many impact investors label this broad thematic area as *financial inclusion*. I deliberately avoid that label because unfortunately, far too many fintech companies "include" more customers but not in a way that improves financial well-being. For example, the lack of savings, for emergency needs or to access certain services, can inhibit those with poor credit scores. Moreover, lenders that provide interest-only loans at 90%+ rates to such financially vulnerable borrowers only burden these individuals with more debt.

Customers prone to higher default rates do pose challenges to the traditional lending model, often resulting in higher service rates. Companies such as Affirm address this challenge with their "Buy now, pay later" business model. Unfortunately, they create another impact risk by enabling imprudent spending capacity. They extend financing beyond nondiscretionary items like medical procedures to cover purchases for high-priced electronics and travel. This access to capital can lead to an increased negative savings rate and eventual need for debt.

While these are viable business models, they may inadvertently create negative impact. Therefore, impact investors focus on providing innovative, profitable, and more positively impactful solutions to serve these customers by identifying levers other than interest rate and incentivizing overspending.

ECONOMIC OPPORTUNITY [171]

One example of this innovation is Jetty, a fintech company with products designed to improve renters' and property managers' financial lives. Rent is a critical portion of household budgets for the roughly 44 million households or 114 million people renting in the United States.[7] The average renter is "rent-burdened," meaning they spend more than 30% of their income on rent. The U.S. Department of Housing and Urban Development highlights that rent-burdened households may have difficulty affording necessities such as food, clothing, transportation, and medical care.

Compounding this burden, renters must apply a significant percentage of their savings to make their deposit payment. For context, the typical deposit requirement is one month's rent (which averages $1,794 in the United States). This imposes considerable stress on financial stability, especially considering that 37% of Americans cannot cover a $400 emergency expense.[8]

Renters face additional financial challenges beyond the deposit. Rent is often due on a particular date each month without regard to when renters are paid. Renters who face timing or other short-term cash flow challenges often chronically pay late fees or take out expensive credit, including payday loans. Renters are also often required to purchase renters insurance on their own and submit proof to the manager, which creates additional cost and administrative burden on renters. Lastly, rent has not traditionally been used to factor into credit scores, making it more difficult to qualify for a mortgage when it is time for a renter to pursue home ownership.

These challenges also affect property managers and owners. They incur friction with collecting, managing, and returning rent and deposits. Unpaid rent impacts property cash flow, and it is expensive and time-consuming should a situation escalate to require an eviction.

Jetty's products make renting a home more flexible and affordable for renters, reduce risk, and increase net operating income for property managers. For example, JettyDeposit provides a more affordable, flexible alternative to traditional cash security deposits. Renters can pay a low, nonrefundable monthly fee instead of a cash security deposit. Through 2023, Jetty has unlocked $279 million for renters that would otherwise be tied up in security deposits. This money can be used to cover other expenses or increase savings levels. For property managers, JettyDeposit reduces bad debt while increasing lease velocity. Jetty also offers products for flexible rent payment (so the due date is more manageable), rent reporting to credit bureaus, and renters insurance.

When we think about economic insecurity, opportunities to address it extend beyond education and financial services. I see professional impact investors finding attractive companies that address gender and racial equity in the workplace, provide reskilling/upskilling and skill-based credentialing, increase the supply of affordable housing that considers the needs of tenants, enable portable benefits for gig workers, and develop insurance products that are more accessible and customizable to enable greater risk management for households that are typically underinsured.

Economic insecurity can also severely impact health, which we will cover next. It is one of the most important themes for impact investors and a massive opportunity set given the number of sectors in which one can approach it.

Chapter Sixteen

Health and Wellness

∼

Nₐₜₒₙₐₗ ₕₑₐₗₜₕCₐᵣₑ ₑₓₚₑₙdᵢₜᵤᵣₑₛ (NHE) in the United States reached $4.5 trillion, or 17.3% of gross domestic product (GDP) in 2022.[1] At $13,493 per capita each year, more than any other country in the world, the high and rising cost of healthcare is a burden on many stakeholders. Of the total NHE, 48% is paid for by federal, state, and local governments, 28% by households, 18% private businesses, and 7% from other private sources.

By some measures, healthcare spending in the United States has paid off in terms of scientific advancements. Our biotechnology industry's development of new drugs and medical devices provides some of the most innovative and cutting-edge medical treatments available in the world. However, there is more to healthcare quality than that.

Despite the level of spending, the United States ranks low in terms of a number of healthcare outcome indicators, including life expectancy, compared to other high-income countries, even when controlling for age and income. According to the Organisation for Economic Co-operation and Development (OECD), much of this is due to avoidable mortality, which is defined as premature deaths among people less than 75 years old that could have been avoided through better prevention and healthcare interventions.[2] Healthcare experts often view this indicator as a window into how effective healthcare systems are with regard to quality and access to care, as both are needed.

Access to healthcare is also a driver of healthcare outcome disparities across race, gender, geography, and income. High costs and insufficient insurance coverage is one barrier, leading patients to forgo necessary care, including preventive screening. Healthcare provider shortages, which are more acute in rural and low-income urban areas, can also lead to worse outcomes. The lack of primary-care physicians is especially detrimental as it leads to unnecessary emergency room visits, which are often more costly and less effective. Other barriers, from transportation to language, add further complexity to bias and discrimination based on race, immigration status, sexual orientation, and other identities. All lead to a gap in healthcare access and outcomes.

There are many goals for impact investors with an interest in health to pursue. Some target the entire health-care system, looking for opportunities to improve efficiency and outcomes or reduce cost and waste. Others seek solutions for specific communities that are most vulnerable and left out of the existing advancements in care. Some aim to improve healthcare outcomes through preventive care, including nutrition and exercise.

These are all noteworthy objectives, and none can independently improve domestic or global healthcare outcomes. The challenges within healthcare are so deeply intertwined among public, private, and nonprofit stakeholders that no single company has a silver bullet to deliver universal, high-quality healthcare. Each of these thematic areas and all the impactful healthcare companies within them together help advance health outcomes. But are all investments in health-care companies impactful, and is there really a difference between how an impact investor selects and manages its investments versus other healthcare investors?

The healthcare sector has certainly been a hot area for venture capital investors in the past two decades.[3] Increasing demand for healthcare services due to an aging population and longer life expectancy create a growing market. Consumer preferences shifting to healthier lifestyles, including a focus on healthier food and adoption of wearable devices to track steps, sleep, and numerous other metrics, all add to the tailwinds. Add healthcare technology innovation to the mix, and it is a ripe opportunity to generate favorable financial returns for a broader group of early-stage venture investors who don't have technical expertise in life sciences.

While healthcare investing still requires expertise in policy and payor dynamics to evaluate businesses, I think most healthcare venture investors stop short of the work impact venture capitalists do when determining what to invest in to drive meaningful impact on the healthcare system or patients. I see companies pitch solutions to pain management, diabetes, sleep disorders, mental health for children, gut health, weight loss, and just about any other ailment. Still, very few of them are evidence-based or can show evidence of improved health outcomes for the populations that need them most through usage of the product or services.

As the consumerization of healthcare has taken off with venture capital funding, more people are willing to pay for subscriptions to apps and software with the promise of improved health. These software-as-a-service revenue models, while potentially profitable, do not address access to care as most are paid out of pocket and require patients to have substantial disposable income.

Private equity investors also have a keen interest in healthcare and have collectively invested more than $1 trillion in the sector over the past decade.[4] It's been one of the strongest performing areas of the market. Historically, investors have focused on specialty hospitals, senior care, and medical devices but recently we've seen an uptick in the acquisitions of physician practices in high-margin specialties, such as dermatology, urology, and ophthalmology.

The investment thesis is straightforward: these fragmented market segments exhibit continued high demand alongside provider shortages. Given the challenges with scale, a private equity fund can acquire practices at a low valuation while bringing professional management, technology enablement, operational improvements, and further acquisitions to boost profits and sell at a higher valuation. While changes *can* produce better healthcare outcomes, it's easy to see how focusing on profitability might erode quality and increase prices. This is a mistake several private equity funds have made to seek a lucrative financial return. I don't believe that enhanced profits and patient outcomes are mutually exclusive, but achieving both requires an intentional and skilled investor to look for and execute changes reinforcing these two goals.

Impact Investing Trends in Health and Wellness

With some perspective on how an investor might identify, due diligence, select, and manage companies with a health impact objective, let's look at some common themes that impact investors have focused on in recent years.

According to the American Medical Association and other associations, racial and ethnic minorities experience a lower quality of healthcare, leading to higher rates of morbidity and mortality than nonminorities.[5] One reason for this trend is lack of access due to the following reasons:

- Bias and mistrust in the healthcare industry that reduces the likelihood of these groups receiving routine medical care
- Lack of education for both patients and providers about resources available to these groups
- Physical proximity to quality healthcare services

Underserved populations include women, LGBTQ identities, neurodiverse individuals, rural communities, and any population that has historically struggled to receive equal access to healthcare. Impact investors wanting to reduce the difference in outcomes look for opportunities to include more of these communities throughout healthcare delivery channels and stages of life.

Alcanza, a clinical research platform targeting diverse clinical trial participants and underserved markets to improve equitable representation in the clinical research space, represents this type of opportunity. Clinical trial populations often do not proportionately represent the populations affected by the disease. For example, a recent Northwestern Medicine study analyzed more than 20,000 clinical trials between 2000 and 2020 and found that women are underrepresented in clinical trials in cardiology, oncology, neurology, immunology, and hematology.[6] This statistic is particularly troubling given that cardiologic and oncologic diseases are among the leading causes of death among women in the United States. Even more striking, a recent analysis of Alzheimer's trials found that while Black people are more prone than white people to develop Alzheimer's disease, they represent only 2% of those included in clinical trials.[7]

Adequate representation is critical in clinical research for various reasons. First, disparities in access to clinical trials prevent minorities from benefiting from advances in science as the trial outcomes are less applicable to the entire population. Second, the efficacy and safety of therapies can vary in different subpopulations. Notably, as evidenced recently by the Moderna COVID vaccine clinical trial, lack of patient recruitment diversity can slow the drug development process.[8] Therefore, equitable access to healthcare and improved outcomes requires representative diversity in trials across various racial, ethnic, gender, and age groups.

However, historically, no clinical trial site network platforms have specifically focused on diversity and increasing representation of minority groups. Private equity firm Martis Capital formed Alcanza, which means *reach* in Spanish, to address this need. Martis utilized a roll-up strategy whereby Martis acquired several clinical trial sites in various geographies to create a business with a national footprint, best-in-class systems, and standard operating procedures that could then differentiate itself through the diversity of its trial participants.

Recruiting and retaining diverse populations into clinical trials is not always straightforward, as specific subpopulations may be hesitant to enroll, may lack the means of adhering to the trial requirements, and may be uneducated about how their involvement in trials may impact their own health or contribute to broader scientific research.

Alcanza's team had to be intentional and thoughtful about engaging with each unique community through culturally competent education, location selection and transportation access, and other practices that would earn trust over time. While Alcanza has been in business for only three years, it is already showing traction with 69% females in their trial populations and 33% minority population within Alcanza's network reach.

The Impact Edge: Win-Win Investing

Alcanza's approach creates a competitive advantage, especially as the U.S. Food and Drug Administration (FDA) signals greater scrutiny of trial populations. This scrutiny may lead competitors to diversify their trial participation.

However, Alcanza has the early-mover advantage, driven by a team willing and interested in thinking critically about how to drive impact and an impact investor behind them to support these efforts. Many of the initiatives Alcanza prioritized from inception did not pay off immediately, nor were they obvious to others in the industry. Similar opportunities exist and are a deep focus of many healthcare impact investors in inclusive care in other settings, from primary-care physicians to specialty practices.

In Part 2, we discussed Array Behavioral Care and its utilization of telemedicine to deliver mental health services to rural communities. This is another example of a first-mover advantage driven by an impact motivation, with a goal of inclusive care and mental health. Impact investors have actively invested in mental health solutions long before it became popular within the broader investment community. No, we didn't reinvent the field; we simply paid attention to experts. Even though insurance companies and other payers dragged their feet on coverage for decades, experts have long claimed that mental and physical health are equal components to health. When the Affordable Care Act included mental and behavioral health as essential health benefits, impact investors were one step ahead in identifying companies that could bring these services to more people.

Impact investors were not alone, but our focus on evidence-based treatments created greater discernment of quality than pure profit-motivated investors. Addiction, for example, is one area of mental health that gained much attention from venture capitalists in the past decade. It's unfortunately a condition with a growing addressable market, especially when considering the numerous types of addictions from substance abuse to opioids and even food. Note that there isn't a hard line between mental and physical health here, as the causes, behaviors, and symptoms of addiction are complex and often come with comorbidities such as anxiety and depression. In fact, chronic medical conditions are three times more expensive to treat when a patient also has a substance abuse disorder.[9] Treatment, therefore, is multifaceted and most importantly should be driven by evidence, not an algorithm based on what an app can identify about you from a quick survey.

Let's look at an example from Impact Engine's portfolio: Workit Health. Robin McIntosh and Lisa McLaughlin cofounded the company in 2015 after experiencing addiction and the flaws in treatment options firsthand and wanted to build a better approach.[10] Therefore, effective care was the core of their mission, and they thus put more resources into building an evidence-based and measurement-based solution to ensure that outcomes are improving. Years of development and continuous improvement created an on-demand, end-to-end virtual solution for addiction treatment that includes all the key components of evidence-based care: medical evaluations with licensed providers, home drug testing, telegroup work, courses, and content. The company's user-centric design is tailored to each patient's individual recovery goals and successfully intervenes and changes members' behaviors before a crisis results.

Workit Health's tech-enabled delivery model reduced the barriers keeping patients from engaging in traditional treatment, including high costs, lack of transportation or childcare, or inability to take time off work. Addiction remains a heavily stigmatized condition, so the privacy of telehealth is a crucial factor for patients seeking discreet care.

Other digital competitors focused more on securing paid advertising to grow revenues as quickly as possible and didn't invest in creating as comprehensive and intentionally designed solutions as Workit Health. Building from a patient-centered design ethos meant refusing to sacrifice clinical quality for rapid growth, which resulted in less early interest from venture investors. In the long run, the company was able to create a competitive advantage by demonstrating greater success with patients.

Workit Health published research on their outcomes in rural populations, which significantly beat those of traditional care and other telehealth programs. The company retained 62% of members at the three-month mark and 99% adhered to their medication. That's huge! Their investment in ensuring and measuring impact has helped them gain traction not only with patients looking for a proven approach but also with commercial health plans and Medicaid plans who appreciate the cost savings in addiction treatment and the whole-person approach informed by clinical quality and lived experience. Building an impactful product from the start vastly increased the growth potential of Workit Health and ensured its accessibility.

This type of win-win is the hallmark of a good impact investment. Great management and execution plus some luck also influence a company's success, but impact can give a company a defensible competitive advantage. This is true in traditional healthcare services and adjacent sectors with the potential to impact health.

Impact Opportunities in Food and Agriculture

The food we eat is another significant driver of health outcomes. While food is not typically paid for in the same way as medical treatments, one would think that companies with better products should also experience these win-wins. "Better for you" food and beverage brands purport to address this opportunity.

However, we should question whether "better for you" food is *good* for you. Let's take oat milk, which saw significant uptake a few years ago when alternative milk products gained mass adoption. Oat milk can be an effective substitute for those with a lactose intolerance or following a vegan diet. But that isn't the only rationale driving customers to buy Swedish-based Oatly, which famously used the tagline "It's like milk, but made for humans."

As sales of Oatly skyrocketed and the company had a successful initial public offering (IPO), Nat Eliason wrote the article "Oatly: the New Coke" about how the company's branding was heavily focused on the health benefits of oat milk and deemphasized the potential health risks of a milk that both contains canola oil and is processed in a way turns the complex carbohydrates in oats into pure sugar.[11] The nutritional profile shows that oat milk has lower protein content than dairy or soy milk and higher calories and carbohydrates than almond and soy milk. While one could argue it's not toxic waste or as bad as smoking a cigarette, is it good for customers substituting it for dairy milk?

If you review Oatly's sustainability report, most of the company's efforts and claims focus not on the health benefits but on how plant-based dairy is less taxing on planet Earth. The food industry, particularly meat and dairy, are undoubtedly significant contributors to greenhouse gas emissions. This comes from the methane emitted from cows as well as feed production, transportation, and other processes in the supply chain. Oatly gets undue credit for positive health impact but has explicitly stated its commitment to sustainability.

In fact, the company put stakes in the ground with goals, including an ambition to "reduce our climate footprint per liter of Oatly produced by 70% and align that ambition with a 1.5 degree climate pathway" by 2029.[12] The company reports its greenhouse gas emissions in a fair amount of depth. It includes strategies for reducing this over time from sustainable ingredient sourcing and renewable energy usage to reducing the waste in packaging and improving transportation-related emissions.

Oatly drives meaningful environmental sustainability impact and yet the grouping of health and environmental impact needs to be more accurate. I don't know if it's intentional on Oatly's part, and Oatly is not alone here. There are many other food companies in the same boat. Beyond Meat is another successful story of a niche food product (plant-based meat substitutes) that achieved mainstream distribution. The company's original impact intent was planetary health, but this was overshadowed by criticism about the nutritional characteristics of its products.

The truth is that innovations in food and agriculture products and services do offer an opportunity to improve human *and* planetary health. Some companies may overstate one or the other in a quest to sell, but the potential is there, and impact investors should take note. Some investors overlook the intersection between health and climate, but I see impact investors who are aware of and more capable of navigating these trade-offs.

Chapter Seventeen

Environmental Sustainability

CLIMATE TECH BECAME ONE of the most prominent investment themes among private markets investors in the past decade, with PricewaterhouseCoopers estimating that deal activity grew from roughly $20 billion in 2013 to nearly $120 billion in 2022.[1] This amounts to 10% of venture capital and private equity investments in 2022, up from approximately 2% in 2013.

The significant demand for solutions to climate change presents an opportunity to deliver outsized financial returns.

Impact investors have an advantage in this area and are poised for market leadership. Many of us have invested in climate tech for more than 20 years, gathering wins and weathering failures, all while gaining a deeper understanding of what solutions will work.

Before climate tech, there was cleantech, which began before and ultimately played victim to the 2008 financial crisis. The release of Al Gore's documentary, *An Inconvenient Truth*, in 2006 sounded the alarm about climate change. Investors took a keen interest in how they could invest in and profit from transformation in how we source and manage energy. While scientists and tree huggers alike talked about the need for renewable energy solutions for years, it took public recognition, notably high energy prices and favorable government policies, to create sufficient demand for clean energy technology for investors to believe that companies offering solutions could succeed. Cambridge Associates estimates that investors poured $25 billion into cleantech companies between 2006 and 2011.[2]

Unfortunately, not all cleantech solutions were fully commercialized, and many required more capital before scaling sufficiently to qualify for venture capital investment. These companies faced additional challenges from the financial crisis, low energy prices, and Chinese companies undercutting prices on solar panels; Cambridge Associates estimates that nearly half of that $25 billion in investment was either lost or impaired.

Impact investors were backers of some of the losing companies in this period. However, most of the dollars lost were invested by generalist funds. These generalists had minimal expertise or experience in these technologies and the sectors (e.g. energy, industrial, and utility) that climate tech companies sell to and/or seek to disrupt. Their opportunistic bet failed due to a changing macroeconomic environment and a need for understanding of a new and growing sector.

What's different today, and why would investors give climate investments a second chance? Most notably, the cost of renewables has substantially declined.[3] Wind, for example, went from a global weighted average levelized cost of electricity that was 95% *higher* than the lowest fossil fuel-fired costs in 2010 to 52% *lower* in 2022. The change in solar energy was even more dramatic. In 2010 it was 710% more expensive than the cheapest fossil fuel–fired solution and dropped to 29% less expensive than fossil fuels in 2022. The unit economics of cleantech solutions became much more compelling as the cost of adjacent technologies, from sensors to software and even business operating costs, also fell.

The skill set and approach of investors in cleantech 2.0 have also changed. First, the number of investment professionals in the field with expertise in sustainability has increased significantly. I've seen this at Chicago Booth. Each year, I divide students in my class up into teams based on their interest areas. Five years ago, 10–20% of my MBA students selected sustainability over health, education, community development, and other domains. This past year, it was 50%. The sophistication of their interest in sustainability has also grown, with teams focused on specific topics such as food and agriculture, decarbonization, and water.

I also see evidence of this shift in the broader private equity (PE)/venture capital (VC) industry. It's hard to attend a traditional industry conference without a panel on sustainability, and shockingly, the speakers actually have experience investing in this space. A decade ago, you'd have folks on stage talking about *why* investing in cleantech should be a priority without deal experience to share. Today the content is much more robust. So, from where did these investors come?

Ironically, some are tenured investors from the oil and gas, power, and industrials sectors. These savvy professionals know that disruptive technologies and companies provide the best opportunities in their sectors. They understand better than any outsider the upstream and downstream energy value chains, the corporate strategic needs, and the unit economics that will make for profitable ventures. This investor profile and the fact that some of the largest and most successful traditional energy funds are launching new funds dedicated to clean technology clearly signal that sustainability has moved mainstream.

When it comes to cleantech investors today, the second shift is in what these investors are willing to invest in. Wiped out and bruised from cleantech 1.0, cleantech 2.0 investors are more wary of taking technology risk. There is a greater focus on software technology that is less capital intensive and can scale more rapidly. However, this is not entirely a positive change because investments in hardware and deep technology are crucial for mitigating climate change. After all, Nest thermostats alone won't save us from our demise.

According to the Intergovernmental Panel on Climate Change, the Industrials sector contributes the largest share of greenhouse gas emissions at 34%. After that, there is food, agriculture, and land use (22%), the built environment (17%), mobility (15%), and energy (12%). Yet from 2013 to 2022, 50% of all PE/VC investments in cleantech went to mobility and 26% to energy with less than 25% to the three largest contributors.[4]

The shortfall of investment dollars relative to sectoral contribution reflects the relative stage of commercialization of technologies within each. For example, mobility includes everything from electric scooters scattered across cities to electric city buses and consumer vehicles. While there continues to be a need to improve battery technology for electric vehicles, we can build and buy electric vehicles at a reasonable price. Within industrials, in contrast, a significant investment in developing new technology in carbon capture and green hydrogen is required before they reach full commercialization stage.

Impact Investors Are Key to Fighting Climate Change

What will it take to fill the funding gap required to meet the goal set by the United Nation's Paris Agreement in 2015 to hold global temperature increases to below 1.5°C above pre-industrial levels? To be honest, I don't think impact investors will save the day. But I also don't think it will happen without impact investors. Let me explain.

The impact investing industry, even though it is growing by $1 trillion, is not large enough to meet the need. The good news is that climate solutions is such a large market opportunity that traditional investors looking for attractive returns have followed impact investors' lead. They see that competitive returns are possible within various asset classes, from fixed income to venture capital and infrastructure finance. However, more than these investments is needed to fill the gap. That's because a full transition to a clean energy economy requires other forces.

- **Consumer behavior:** Consumers/people have to make behavioral changes, from "reduce, reuse, recycle" to choosing products and services that emit fewer green-house gasses and create less waste. This will not always cost less or even the same. Luckily, Gen Z and

Alpha are showing signs of this being a preference given their awareness of the long-term costs of choosing unsustainable products to both the planet and our health.

- **Governmental intervention:** Federal and local governments around the world will need to continue to employ creative incentives and regulations to motivate businesses to do better. This includes managing the environmental impact of their manufacturing processes, supply-chain partners, product packaging and transportation, and product end-of-life attributes.

I became interested in the investment community as a force for change because I felt that the government was not doing enough to manage and incentivize corporations. Consumer engagement also fell short. I never thought investors would be the holy grail and that we could abandon other attempts but rather serve as the third leg of a stool essential to unlock all the benefits and keep in check for-profit companies. If done right, the power of a profit motive can truly unleash the innovation required to solve climate change. That leads to an important interplay between these actors. As companies develop innovations, governments can more effectively regulate behavior and incentivize adoption, and consumers can make informed choices.

The Climate Investment Opportunity: Energy Transition, Resource Efficiency, and Adaptation

Finally, I want to briefly cover the three broad themes and company examples I see within environmental sustainability so that you know where to look for the best opportunities: energy transition, resource efficiency, and adaptation.

Energy transition includes investments in renewables and the infrastructure necessary for the successful transmission of renewables. SER Capital Partners, a middle market private equity impact fund, created Perfect Power to acquire, develop, and operate renewable energy generation and battery energy storage assets.[5] The company focuses entirely on resources to help create a carbon-free electrical grid. Renewable energy generation can't replace fossil fuels without the ability to store energy.

Energy transition also requires electrification of transportation, homes, and industrial processes. Not every home can support a solar panel on its roof, due to installation cost or location attributes such as sun exposure, yet the market for community solar is expected to grow to a $81 billion market by 2030.[6]

Decarbonization is another opportunity through carbon capture and management. Growth equity investor Carbon Direct Capital focuses on this theme. The firm invested in

Twelve, a San Francisco-based technology company that makes the chemicals, materials, and fuels from air with its revolutionary carbon transformation technology.[7] Twelve replicates photosynthesis at industrial scale. Similar to a plant in nature, Twelve's patented process transforms CO_2 into useful outputs with just water and renewable energy as additional inputs. This allows the company to enter end markets for products that are made from fossil fuels, such as fuels and chemicals.

Resource Efficiency plays a central role in tackling climate change, including decreasing the amount of energy used in order to lower GHG emissions and other pollutants. San Diego–based Measurable built a sustainability performance platform for real estate managers, owners, and operators that provides actionable insights to make changes to improve the energy efficiency of buildings.

Another key area of sustainability centers around improving water management. As the effects of climate change rise, as many as 800 million additional people are expected to live in urban areas under severe water stress compared to today, resulting in lack of access to water for drinking, washing, cleaning, and industrial applications. Solutions that can decrease our water demand, increase our water supply, or treat and reuse wastewater more effectively can help address this issue.

Finally, waste is a significant indicator of whether resources are being used efficiently. Global waste generation is expected to increase 70% by 2050, faster than any other environmental pollutant.[8] It is estimated that implementing effective waste management practices at scale could cut up to 15% of GHG emissions globally.[9] Companies that power the circular economy and efficiently use the planet's resources are critical. Matsmart, a Swedish online food retailer, sells surplus food that would otherwise be at risk of being discarded. Their food is sold at a significant discount (think Aldi meets Instacart!), addressing food insecurity while also reducing food waste.

Climate Adaptation focuses on how society can adapt to the effects of climate change, such as heatwaves, droughts, wildfires, and floods that occur with greater frequency and magnitude. It's estimated that more than 40% of the world's population is already affected by moderate to severe climate hazards.[10] We must rapidly develop and implement solutions to help our society become more resilient to these changes and to avoid mounting loss of life, biodiversity, and infrastructure.

Climate risk intelligence platforms that analyze and manage risks due to flood, fire, heat, and drought for sectors including insurers, financial services, corporations, and land owners represent one approach. These tools can help organizations translate historical, current, and predictive information about both our natural and built systems into actionable business intelligence. This allows insurers to incorporate physical climate risks into their policies and encourages institutions to invest in building resilience. It also enables the financial services sector to offer better financing rates to borrowers who disclose and reduce their emissions and make progress on their sustainability goals.

Solutions that help growers transition to regenerative practices can also help make our food systems more resilient. Controlled environment agriculture has the potential to shorten the food supply chain and better meet the needs of food deserts, all while requiring less water and land than traditional agriculture. Gotham Greens was founded in 2009 when cofounders Viraj Puri and Eric Haley teamed up with greenhouse expert Jenn Frymark to build and operate sustainable greenhouses to grow leafy greens and herbs year-round.[11] Their indoor farming facilities are sun and wind-powered, climate-controlled, and utilize data-driven, efficient production systems to create high-yielding farms that use less energy, less land, and less water than other farming techniques.

In addition to investing *in* solutions to create environmental sustainability, there is also the option to do the opposite—divest or sell investments in fossil fuel companies. Today, more than 1,600 institutions with more than $40 trillion have divested fossil fuel companies from their stock portfolios.[12] Much like the apartheid divestment movement, it is led by faith-based organizations and universities including Harvard

University and many Catholic institutions after the urging of Pope Francis. Pension funds (e.g. New York State Common Retirement Fund), governmental entities (e.g. Norwegian Sovereign Wealth Fund), and philanthropic pools of capital (e.g. Ford Foundation) have also made divestment pledges.

The theory of change for fossil fuel divestment is that it will mobilize public pressure, reduce capital availability, or increase the cost of capital, creating operating challenges for companies. Unfortunately, when you sell stock shares of a company, someone else buys them. But perhaps the public nature of divestment can influence change within corporations or legislatures, as we saw with apartheid. Alternatively, could owning shares of fossil fuel stocks create an opportunity to create change within the boardroom?

Chapter Eighteen

Public Markets

$\sim$

As discussed in Chapter 6, there are meaningful differences between environmental, social, and governance (ESG) and impact investing. While much of the activity in public markets is categorized as ESG management with little intention or know-how about creating impact, deploying impact management tools with public companies has significant potential for those investors willing to learn and apply new skills.

There are a few unique characteristics of investing in public versus private companies. First, it is difficult to become a significant shareholder unless you are a very large investor and/or have a concentrated portfolio. The top five share-holders of Microsoft, for example, are the largest index fund managers: Vanguard, State Street, BlackRock, Fidelity, and T Rowe Price. Looking at some of the other largest companies, you'll occasionally see Berkshire Hathaway or activist investors like Elliott Management, Carl Icahn, and Pershing Square. Unless you are one of these investors, engaging and influencing public companies in the same way a venture or private equity investor can is difficult. Put it this way—writing a $10 million check into a startup will get you a board seat but won't even register as a notable event for a public company.

Second, buying and selling shares of public companies both occur on a secondary market. When a company's shares are listed on the New York Stock Exchange or Shanghai Stock Exchange, *investing* just means buying shares from an existing investor with no capital inflow to the company or specified terms aside from potential voting rights. In private markets, most transactions are primary, meaning the investment goes to the company. It also means that the terms of the investment, from the price to certain structural rights, are unique to each transaction. Secondary transactions are also possible, for example where one private equity fund buys the company from another. Still, even then, it's usually to facilitate a new chapter or stage for the company that involves growth or improved operations. These transactions are also privately negotiated and include terms unavailable in public markets.

Third, the duration of investment is binary in public markets. Index funds and asset owners tend to hold their shares for many years and sometimes decades. Yet there are also short-term quantitative traders, and even high-frequency traders, simply playing a game of arbitrage where ownership may last a few months or even just a few seconds. Some mutual funds and hedge funds may have holding periods between these extremes, but it's still much shorter than the consistent duration of 3–10 years for venture and private equity investors. These varying time horizons create opportunities and challenges for investors with an impact lens. For example, proxy voting and engagement may become more important for index investors (essentially permanent capital).

Finally, and perhaps most importantly, the investment thesis or "how you make money" in public markets typically focuses solely on price arbitrage. There are value investors who seek to invest when they believe a company's share price is lower than its true value and sell once that delta is narrowed. Similarly, growth investors invest believing that the company's future growth is not reflected in the current price. Unless you are an activist investor, it's uncommon for value or growth investors to have a thesis around their value-add to support the company with a specific initiative that will increase its value. The premise relies more on mispricing.

Therefore, while board directors or executives at public companies have a duty to all shareholders, they may not be interested in the opinions of or involvement from public stock investors, especially as these investors typically lack useful operating skill sets. This is the opposite of private markets, where an investor's ideas and track record of value creation can be what wins them the deal and differentiates them from other potential investors.

We learned in Part One that the key ingredients of impact investing are intentionality, including a theory of change and supporting diligence to understand and believe in the potential impact; measurement to validate and manage impact as it's being created; and management, often through community and engagement, terms and incentives, and legal structures. Some but not all of these are possible within the constraints of public markets investing outlined earlier.

There is no reason that investing in public companies can't carry intentionality with it. If you want to pick a stock or build a portfolio of stocks with a goal of reducing greenhouse gas emissions, it's possible to select companies whose primary business is driving improvement in energy transition, resource efficiency, or climate adaptation. Alternatively, you could select companies committed to improving their operations and supply chain to meaningfully reduce their carbon footprint by utilizing climate solutions.

Access to considerable information in the public domain allows an investor to conduct due diligence on public companies. This includes annual reports, 10-Ks, impact reports, press releases, and news articles about the company,

Glass Door and other employee reviews, sell-side analyst reports, and even your own use of the company's products and services. You can listen to the management team's earnings calls or call an investor relations representative to ask your questions. You can use these inputs to develop a sound theory of change.

Measurement of impact in public companies is complex but possible. Whereas your logic model may suggest outputs to measure impact key performance indicators (KPIs), these are usually for specific products or services. Public companies often have many divisions or business lines with hundreds or thousands of products. You would also have to carry significant ownership to convince a public company to measure impact for you. The good news is that more companies are attempting to measure and disclose ESG metrics, such as the IFRS Foundation standards referenced in Chapter 3. It's plausible that a target company's disclosures include a meaningful metric that an impact investor could track to evaluate improvement over time.

The rub comes with the last component, management, and "additionality," a heavily debated word among professional impact investors that presumes the impact would not have occurred without the investor. As the mainstream investment community noticed that impactful companies make great investments, investors' efforts to support a company's impact initiatives creates the basis of additionality. These efforts may include advocating for inclusive hiring practices and vetoing the company's sale to a competitor that isn't mission-aligned.

Many argue that additionality requires proof of impact management. Still, unless you are a major shareholder, it's difficult to embark on this type of engagement and management with a public company. Critics of impact investing in public markets point out that most investors are not large enough to influence or help a public company, and thus, there is no additionality.

Yet, while many of the tools we discussed for impact management in Chapter 12 are off the table with public company investment, one can influence management by employing mechanisms specific to public companies. The first is proxy voting, or when shareholders are asked to vote on certain issues the company is considering. This includes approving board directors, mergers and acquisitions, and executive compensation plans. Impact investors can vote based on their intended social or environmental goals. For example, if a board member does not support efforts to achieve a net zero carbon emissions goal, investors can vote against approving the board member when their term is up for renewal. It's true that a small shareholder's vote alone won't sway a decision, but more impact-oriented matters are coming up for vote and gaining traction with shareholders.

A shareholder even has a mechanism to put a matter up for a vote. This is called a *shareholder resolution*, which is presented and voted on during a company's annual shareholder meeting. If approved by the majority of shareholders, in the U.S. market it is a nonbinding suggestion to the board. Even though directors don't have to abide by the advice given in the resolution, it creates a record and can often influence companies to take action.

The year 2023 saw a record number of 513 environmental and social shareholder resolutions.[1] It has been on a consistent uptick since 2017, although this past year saw a drop in the average support for these proposals to 23% from 31% in 2022. This may stem from ESG backlash as political disagreements have become entangled, and there were even some "anti-ESG" proposals. It's also possible that the decline was driven by companies improving their ESG efforts and disclosures, which rendered many resolutions redundant.

What types of resolutions do impact-motivated investors propose? In recent years, proposals for climate disclosure or setting emission reduction targets have been among the most common. Related resolutions ask for increased disclosures for climate transition plans, fossil fuel financing, and climate lobbying. Diversity, equity, and inclusion (DEI) also became a common shareholder proposal in recent years, with specific requests for racial equity or civil rights audits. Other common topics include health and safety issues, labor rights, operations in countries with human rights violations, and, more recently, reproductive rights and data privacy.

So far, we've covered the possibilities for impact as an equity investor in public companies. There are also approaches to creating impact in public fixed-income markets, even where an investor does not have voting rights.

Municipal (or "muni") bonds, or those issued by public municipalities from cities to schools and hospitals, are ripe for creating impact. The reason is that the proceeds from these bonds are often designated for specific communities and purposes. Investors wanting to create impact from this portion of their portfolio can look for funds that intentionally target not just water and sewer muni bonds, for example, but those to replace lead pipes or build climate-resilient infrastructure. Similarly, bonds can fund nutritious free lunches for low-income school districts or to create mental healthcare access for students.

While muni bonds are like stocks, in that they generally trade in the secondary market, muni bond funds have greater access to and more commonly use the primary or original issuance market. Moreover, the relative size and liquidity profile of bonds offered by smaller municipalities means that trading affects pricing more directly.

However, there is a new and growing segment of the fixed-income market that creates even more additionality—green bonds. These bonds are issued exclusively for projects with a positive environmental impact, such as a renewable energy development or sustainable buildings. Capital raised from these bonds is typically earmarked for the specific green project, but the issuer's entire balance sheet backs it. The issuer could be a government related organization; for example, the first green bond was issued in 2007 by the European Investment Bank, which is the European Union's lending arm,[2] and the following year the World Bank issued the second green bond.[3]

Fannie Mae, the U.S. government-backed mortgage financier, is a large issuer of green bonds that help finance homes and rental communities that meet energy- and water-saving standards. For example, Fannie Mae's Single-Family Green Mortgage Backed Securities are made up of mortgages backed by newly constructed single-family residential homes with ENERGY STAR® certifications that meet or exceed the national program requirements for ENERGY STAR 3.0 Certified Homes. These homes are, on average, 20% more efficient than single-family homes built to code.[4]

Corporations can also issue green bonds. In 2019, PepsiCo issued a 30-year, $1 billion green bond with proceeds designated to build a more sustainable food system by supporting PepsiCo's investments in sustainable plastics and packaging, decarbonization of its operations and supply chain and water sustainability.[5] Pepsi's green bond website includes specifics about projects the capital funded and the impact created.

Currently, annual green bond issuance totals about $500 billion, and many come with the benefits of tax exemptions or tax credits.[6] While it's promising to see such a large market development in the past 15 years that is directly tied to projects that will drive a more sustainable planet, there is also a need for accountability to ensure issuers are not greenwashing. Social impact bonds, which we'll cover next, take a similar approach but with financial returns tied to social performance.

Social Impact Bonds

Pᴇʀꜰᴏʀᴍᴀɴᴄᴇ-ʙᴀꜱᴇᴅ ᴄᴏɴᴛʀᴀᴄᴛꜱ, ᴏʀ ꜱᴏᴄɪᴀʟ impact bonds, require social programs to achieve predetermined impact goals before receiving payment. It certainly sounds like the holy grail for impact investors. However, the complexity and costs required to execute these investments successfully limit the feasible use cases. Experts have written books dedicated to this topic, so we will cover these market mechanisms only at a high level to understand where and when impact investors should consider them.

Social impact bonds are intended to provide greater funding for high-impact interventions for the most vulnerable communities that often don't see adequate investment. This public–private partnership enables greater funding levels because of the performance-based approach. It is especially valuable in situations where government spending thus far hasn't produced outcomes and, if left unaddressed, are costly to society. Public support in these situations can be hard to garner despite the need. Providing programs designed for the exact demographic, with clear metrics to track success, gives everyone more assurance.

Social Finance U.K. created the first social impact bond in 2010 to fund interventions for inmates leaving Peterborough Prison, with the hope of reducing instances of reoffending and returning to prison.[1] As you may recall from Chapter 2, the U.K. government was interested in for-profit investments to address societal issues during that time, and Social Finance was one of their early investments. Here is how Social Finance U.K. set up their inaugural performance-based contract:

> Foundation and private investors, including the Rockefeller Foundation, provided £5m capital to support offenders before and after their release from prison. This was conducted through One Service, an organization dedicated to ex-prisoners with social workers and programs to help with employment, housing, substance abuse

challenges, debt, family dynamics, and other important elements of reintegration.

If reoffending decreased by 7.5% across the pilot compared to the national control group, investors would be paid back their principal plus an additional return. Government savings generated from lower reconviction rates would fund this return. If results were not achieved, investors could see a partial or full capital loss. Essentially, the government paid for success, and investors took the downside risk if programs did produce the intended social outcomes.

The program included two cohorts with 2,000 participants over five years, and Social Finance U.K. reported that the social impact bond program had reduced reoffending rates by 8.4% compared to the control group. The investors received full repayment of principal plus a roughly 3% annualized return over the period.

Since Peterborough, more than $750 million has been raised for nearly 300 "pay for success" contracts.[2] Employment and job training, health, child and family welfare, and education make up the majority of policy focus areas. While a heavy concentration of social impact bonds is coming out of the U.K. and Europe, more than 35 countries worldwide have participated.

While the market has grown, it's fairly small compared to the *annual* green bond issuance of $500 billion. Why is that? For one, these investments offer fairly low returns with considerable risk. Foundations and other philanthropic organizations are the primary investors willing to take on the risk of the program not being successful for the upside potential of low single-digit returns. Moreover, it usually takes a few, if not several, years to know if an intervention is successful. Most investors expect returns to increase with holding periods, so it further limits the number of interested investors.

The complexity and costs of structuring these contracts present another challenge. They require a government or quasi-government agency, like a development finance institution, which means there is often a lengthy approval process.

Goal thresholds often need to be thought through adequately. These targets need to be meaningful, as in the level of change is significant enough, but also achievable and clearly defined. This often requires expertise and research.

Assuming the investors and sponsor agree on the goals, you must have the resources to measure accurately. Typically a nonprofit or social sector organization with expertise is selected to conduct the program. The measurement agent must be independent, given the potential for conflict of interest. Finding and selecting them takes time and resources, and these organizations do not always have the capacity to conduct measurements. All of this adds up to a lengthy, complex, and hard-to-replicate process, considering the various parties (investors, sponsors, service providers) vary each time. A social impact bond targeting refugee employment support in France differs wildly from one focused on reskilling homeless youth in the United States or low-income housing in Nigeria.

That said, many of the social impact bonds that have matured have been successful. It's a savvy approach to transfer risk from the public (taxpayers and government) to the private sector (investors and philanthropists) in a way that incentivizes achieving measurable impact. Scale is also not always the measure of success. Highly tailored interventions may be hard to replicate, but the impact on the lives affected and ripple effects can be significant and worthwhile. Social impact bonds also satisfy a deep hope I think many have for impact investing to be embedded in a structure that makes it impossible to change over time. It may not be the structure for all impact investments, but it's a proof point and has created a desire from the impact investing ecosystem to explore other structures.

Chapter Twenty

Alternative
Ownership Structures

❧

WHAT IF THERE WAS no need for impact investors? If corporate governance mechanisms inspired, incentivized, and supported companies to use their resources for good, we wouldn't need those tools from impact investors, right?

Everything we've covered in this book assumes that investors' economic and governance rights are intertwined. If you invest, you have a say in how a company is run (e.g. as a board director or through proxy votes) and get a share of profits, right? But if you work at a company, shouldn't you also have a say and be rewarded when the company does well? What about customers or other stakeholders?

Traditional ownership structures, such as common or preferred stock, have advantages. Providing investors with economic and governance rights rewards risk-taking and provides some control or checks and balances over management. Who would risk their capital with no economic upside potential and no ability to vote on important decisions like the sale of a company? Large functioning markets exist because of those rights. Take them away, and I don't think as many people will participate in the stock market or venture capital.

This model also comes with drawbacks. It promotes short-termism, as the time horizon for investors (anywhere from seconds for high-frequency traders to several years for PE funds) is misaligned with companies that have no set or needed expiration date. This means investors can make decisions that improve profitability in the next year yet set the company up for bankruptcy years later. It can also breed disenfranchisement from employees, who may work tirelessly and see no upside when a company does well while watching investors profit massively.

It also negatively affects society due to the concentration of wealth generation. The wealth potential of an owner who participates in profits far outstrips what a wage earner or even someone on a salary can earn. There have been numerous studies showing that high levels of income inequality hamper economic growth and also weaken democracy.[1]

Alternative ownership structures represent an exciting area of growth for impact investors. These structures alter investors' economic and governance rights to include other stakeholders. There are many possibilities as terms are privately negotiated, but let's look at the legal structures that are most commonly used.

The most common form of employee ownership is the employee stock ownership plan (ESOP), a retirement plan that allows employees to share in the ownership interest of the company where they work. Like a pension plan, employees receive the profits when they retire or leave the company, yet they do not have to pay to participate in their ownership. Any and all employees can be included in an ESOP, from the chief executive officer (CEO) to the janitor. ESOPs have a number of tax advantages, the most significant of which is that they do not pay federal corporate taxes. When an owner of a business sells its interests to an ESOP, she also does not pay taxes on the gains.

ESOPs have existed since the 1960s, and there are more than 6,000 plans in existence today.[2] However, it's only recently that impact investors began seeing them as a tool to address wealth inequality. More than two million business owner exits are approaching as Baby Boomers retire, which some call a silver tsunami, creating an opportunity to convert thousands of companies to ESOPs instead of selling to traditional private equity or a competitor.

There is also a strong business case for employee ownership. Research suggests that companies owned by their employees, as opposed to its founders, executives, or external investors, demonstrate fewer layoffs, improved wages and benefits, and significantly increased wealth-building opportunities for workers at *all* income levels. For example, the average ESOP account in 2018 was valued at $134,000—a significant nest egg considering that 70% of Americans have less than $1,000 in savings.[3]

A study conducted by the National Center for Employee Ownership found that after becoming ESOPs, firms saw sales, employment, and productivity grow more than 2% faster per year than otherwise would have been expected.[4] A Rutgers University study showed similar results, in addition to evidence that employee-owned firms were more likely than peer firms to survive downturns or other routine causes of business failure.[5]

There are numerous examples of viable, profitable employee-owned companies that have benefitted from this ownership structure, including easily recognized consumer-facing companies such as Eileen Fisher and Publix. Our team at Impact Engine began looking in 2021 for opportunities to convert more companies to ESOPs. Zero Waste Recycling (ZWR) was our first. The Charlotte, North Carolina–based company is a full-service, one-stop solution provider that helps manufacturers recycle or divert up to 100% of their operational waste. The potential to create measurable wealth for ZWR's employees, more than 75% of whom are BIPOC and/or LMI, is compelling. The conversion transferred 100% of the company to the hands of all the employees, not just senior management. If the growth plan for the next several years plays out, these employees will share in meaningful profits. The risk/reward is also well-balanced. If the company does not do well, employees miss out but never have to pay to participate in this upside.

So how does an investor participate in such a conversion if the company is entirely owned by its employees? Investors can provide the financing of the ESOP's purchase from its seller. In the case of Zero Waste, Impact Engine joined a syndicate of investors, led by Mosaic Capital Partners, that provided a loan to the new ESOP to buy out the founders. To ensure that ESOP conversations are done in a way that does not harm the employees or business, there are several parties involved to represent the employees from a trustee to valuation experts. Importantly, ESOP-owned companies can use tax savings to pay back the loan. Depending on the appropriate interest rate, warrants, and other structures to create upside potential, it is possible to generate a private equity–like return from such conversions.

An employee ownership trust (EOT) is essentially a trust that owns a business, but the purpose of the trust must include the well-being of the company's employees. It is similar to an ESOP in that the business operates with the employees' interests in mind, but an EOT has more variability in how employees benefit. It may be through profit-sharing, but it can also be more general guidance to consider their needs. EOTs are not tax-advantaged but are less costly to create and administer because they are also not regulated like ESOPs.

Cooperatives are another form of ownership that shakes up the role of investors. Here, people who produce or use the company's products, supplies, or services own the company and also share in profits. I know that your local grocery story co-op comes to mind right now, but did you know that Ace Hardware (owned by its retailers), REI (owned by member customers), Associated Press (owned by its newspaper and broadcast members), EqualExchange (owned by workers), and Land O' Lakes (owned by producers) are all co-ops?

Co-op members have voting and economic rights, which encourages members to contribute to profits and make decisions that will benefit the business. Being economically tied provides other benefits, such as collective bargaining when buying from suppliers. An Ace Hardware retailer, for example, can get lower prices with higher-volume purchases. They also benefit from a recognizable national brand, which is how these small, locally owned retailers survived the rise of Home Depot. Sharing distribution channels, like the grocery stores that sell Land O' Lakes products and EqualExchange coffee beans, is another benefit and allows local dairy and coffee producers and workers to benefit from the success of the shared brands.

All of this is great for keeping the profits and decision rights in the hands of those operating businesses. It certainly can reduce the principal-agent problem, which occurs when there is a conflict of interest between the agent (workers) taking action and the principal (owner). ESOP, EOT, and co-op structures also allow the agents to be the principals. However, there is another approach that goes beyond this relationship to incorporate the company's purpose directly into its legal structure.

A perpetual purpose trust (PPT) is a noncharitable trust created to benefit an explicit purpose, instead of a human beneficiary, in perpetuity. The purpose can be to benefit employees, poverty alleviation, the planet, or a number of other causes. Contrast this to the commonly held misbelief that the sole purpose of a corporation is to maximize shareholder value!

How does a PPT operate, and how is it governed? Let's share an example to make the explanation easier to understand. Matt Kreutz started Firebrand Artisan Breads in 2008.[6] His successful baked goods company employs the formerly incarcerated and homeless. Matt saw an opportunity to create good jobs for this vulnerable population, while also solving the common challenge of demanding work with long hours and high turnover in the food service industry. His investment in training programs creates opportunities for leadership roles and provides an inclusive culture where employees are encouraged to bring their full selves to the workplace, which has helped fuel the company's success.

A few years ago, Matt wanted to raise capital to launch a line of packaged goods. Even among impact investors, he struggled with the idea of an investor helping the company and then exiting. Matt wanted an investor who was aligned with his mission as well as his long-term view. As he explored different options, he found that a PPT could accomplish both objectives.

The Firebrand PPT's defined purposes are as follows[7]:

1. Preserve Firebrand's independence and values, and promote the Company's mission of creating great jobs, shared value, and thriving communities.
2. Protect employee and community participation in the governance of the trust and board of directors.
3. Operate the Company for the benefit of the Stakeholders rather than profit maximization and shareholder return, while acknowledging the necessity of financial and competitive security for the long-term viability of the enterprise.

4. Prioritize hiring people who are formerly incarcerated, homeless, or otherwise have high barriers to entering the workforce.

5. Protect the inclusion of employee and community participation in profit-sharing.

Who oversees the company to ensure that this purpose is fulfilled? A trust stewardship committee that includes Matt, select employees, and community members manages this responsibility. The committee appoints board members to represent the trust's ownership in governing the company.

The company's ownership consists of 33% by the Firebrand PPT, 30% by Matt, 8% by employees, and the remainder by mission-aligned investors who facilitated the significant sale to the PPT. The investors played a critical role as co-conspirators in creating an alternative to traditional economic and voting rights. Specifically, they agreed to receive 90% of Firebrand's distributed profits until they achieved two times their principal while 10% would go to employees. Once two times is achieved, profits are distributed based on ownership.

After seven years, investors can redeem their investment at either two times their original purchase price or the fair market value minus any distributions made after the profit flip. After 10 years, the company can also force redemption. When the company buys back those shares, they will be allocated to the PPT to increase employees' ownership and profit share. This structure ensures that employees are part of the company's economic benefits in perpetuity. The trust-appointed board of directors, including employee representatives, governs this process.

If this seems too complicated to be realistic for a larger company, consider the fact that Patagonia's founder Yves Chouinard converted his ownership to a PPT in 2022 to benefit climate protection and land preservation.[8] Patagonia used a different structure with two entities, the Patagonia Perpetual Purpose Trust and the nonprofit Holdfast Collective. Each has separate voting and economic rights. Chouinard sold only 2% of his stock to the PPT, yet these represent 100% of the voting rights. In contrast, 98% went to the nonprofit, but these shares have no voting rights.

In other words, the PPT is responsible for managing the company for the purpose of the planet and can decide annually whether reinvesting profits into the operating business or distributing dividends to the nonprofit will best serve the mission. While this requires sound judgment from the trust—and may not always be perfect—it does well to structurally address the conflict of interest between someone who controls economic and voting rights if their mission is to protect the planet.

Impact investing with traditional ownership structures is just an imperfect market mechanism to address this conflict of interest. When a founder wants to create impact and is backed by investors who want the same thing, the conflict is reduced only as long as both the principal and agent remain aligned. As leadership expands from the founder to include a C-suite and middle management and then the investor base changes hands, how likely is it that impact goals will be shared?

Culture and incentives can help no doubt. Tying bonuses and other forms of compensation to hitting impact key performance indicators (KPIs) can motivate people. But if we can create a large investor base looking for PPTs willing to share ownership and economics with employees and other stakeholders, the power of impact investing will be even greater. It's the most exciting chapter of impact investing and is only getting started!

Much like the ESG movement created the understanding and backdrop for impact investing to thrive, impact investing is creating that backdrop for alternative ownership structures to become the norm. While policymakers have a significant role to play, in creating tax advantages like ESOPs, investors also have an opportunity to make this happen now. Investors can prove to policymakers that these companies are better for society and that they should provide incentives to promote their creation.

Conclusion

————————— ❧ —————————

Is it just me, or does your heart race when you think about a perpetual purpose trust becoming the norm? I was on the edge of my seat as I wrote the last chapter, bursting with excitement about the possibility that *ownership*, the epitomic word of capitalism, could be the lever that unlocks the most enduring impact.

I hope you've seen that impact investing is not just another asset class. It is the linchpin to creating new kinds of value in companies that deliver financial, social, and environmental benefits to investors alongside the communities where we live and work. Investors can use compelling impact management strategies to build more resilient, valuable companies. Once you put an impact lens on your investment glasses, you'll see it's like going from a basic cell phone to a smartphone. There is so much more depth and possibility. And once you see all that is possible, not considering impact investment strategies will seem inadequate, perhaps even reckless.

That said, I don't think we're headed to a world where all investments will be impact investments. Unfortunately, there will always be a buyer for a company that is purely focused on financial gain at all costs. There are also no perfect companies, as impact is multidimensional. A business, for example, can be capable of driving significant impact for its employees while having real limitations with its products.

I am hopeful about the development of tools to assess all the dimensions of impact for any investment in your portfolio. This will empower investors to make informed decisions. Professional investors already consider liquidity, taxes, and many other factors. They are trained to evaluate trade-offs and build portfolios to optimize multiple needs. Consider risk versus return. No one invests in a short-term investment-grade bond fund thinking there is less risk and higher return potential than the S&P 500 over the long term. Impact is just one more thing for them to consider. As one of the industries with the highest compensation levels, shouldn't we expect them to use their skills to improve society?

I believe we're in an age of codification, which will normalize the terminology, approaches, and expectations of the various impact strategies. It's analogous to the gestation period that the hedge fund industry went through where investors began to understand that a long/short equity fund and systematic macro trading fund had very different return, risk, and liquidity expectations even though they are both hedge funds. As the world is educated about impact investing, the data will inform us of what to expect regarding returns and impact.

The rapid advances make some people nervous, but change doesn't have to mean that the old guard in the investment industry dies. They can put their sword down and embrace new possibilities. Many are doing this. TPG, one of the largest private equity firms in the world, manages $18 billion within its impact-driven Rise Funds.[1] I'm sure there are many motivations for starting and growing that area of their business—from personal desire to employee interest to client demand. They're not the only ones, as just about any asset manager today either has or is considering an impact investment offering.

However, we also experience pushback from outside of the investment community. Some politicians view impact investing as an attack on capitalism instead of the most beautiful version of it. Some corporate executives also contribute to the backlash. I'm not surprised, as this is a classic extinction burst like toddlers have when behavior changes are introduced and expected. There is a sudden increase in that behavior before it eventually stops. The leaders publicly throw fits and act without considering the effects on other people and the planet, knowing that that won't be possible soon enough.

As I write this book, regulators are introducing new environmental, social, and governance (ESG) and impact disclosure frameworks for public companies, registered funds, and advisors. They probably won't get it right the first time, and there will be further backlash about the added costs and burden of such requirements. I have faith that with input and iteration, rules will help. Progress not perfection, right? Don't we all appreciate that audits must follow Generally Accepted Accounting Principles (GAAP) rather than allowing each company to determine how to manage their books?

I believe this generation of impact investors will usher in a new era of capitalism with or without regulations. There is enormous talent in the business and finance communities itching to do more with their energy and abilities than to only make themselves richer. They want to engage professionally in a way that aligns with their inner truth. The culture of capitalism and finance (more than the concepts themselves) previously created a dearth of opportunity for them. The root word of integrity is *integer*, which means "whole" in Latin. To have integrity means that you think and act in a way that brings your whole self to the plate. When you cut off your values when managing a business or making an investment decision, you are not acting with integrity. And I think we're all sick of this.

I have rarely met a finance professional who is only out for themselves. Most are just as caring as teachers, doctors, and other vocations viewed as socially beneficial. We must let go of the myth that businesspeople are bad and selfish to avoid creating a vicious self-fulfilling prophecy. Let's set a higher bar and inspire a higher calling. We won't thrive as a society, and capitalism won't make it, if we entrust only public servants, nonprofit leaders, and philanthropists to solve our greatest challenges. We need everyone to be part of the solution.

The investment office of endowments, pensions, or any other investor—large or small—possesses enormous power. It's not just the government that can influence how corporations behave. Investors can create change and learn and iterate more quickly. It's what drew me into this industry. But it can't have that kind of change until we change the expectation that one's portfolio must consider values. People from different backgrounds and with diverse points of view belong in the investment office. And more than a risk-return analysis belongs in an investment memo.

The time is now. And now that you've read this book, you have the power to be in the driver's seat when it comes to directing *your* capital to impact. Consider your bank and who it lends your deposits to. Look for impact options in your 401k plan. Call your financial advisor and ask how the mutual funds they've selected vote their proxies for shareholder resolutions. Ask your employer what their objectives are for creating impact. And when people say no, try to talk to you like you don't know what you're doing, or attempt to scare you into believing that this will cost you something, it's time to push back or walk away. The impact investing industry has grown to more than $1 trillion in assets under management because of one very big voice: clients. That's you! You are more powerful than you think.

Notes

Preface

1. Rodin, J., & Brandenburg, M. (2014). *The Power of Impact Investing: Putting Markets to Work for Profit and Global Good.* Wharton Digital Press.
2. Global Impact Investing Network. (2022). (rep.). Global Impact Investing Network (GIIN) Estimates Worldwide Impact Investing Market Size to be USD $1.164 Trillion in an Industry Milestone (pp. 1–3).

Chapter One

1. Statista. (n.d.). (rep.). Lobbying in the US – Statistics and Facts
2. Global Impact Investing Network. (2018). (rep.). Roadmap for the Future of Impact Investing: Reshaping Financial Markets.
3. About acumen. Acumen. (2023, February 22). https://acumen.org/about

4. Grameen Foundation. Muhammad Yunus. (2024). https://grameen foundation.org/about-us/leadership/muhammad-yunus

5. About. Double Bottom Line Investors. (n.d.). https://www.dbl.vc/about

6. Global Impact Investing Network (GIIN). The Rockefeller Foundation. (2023, May 2). https://www.rockefellerfoundation.org/from-the-archives/global-impact-investing-network-giin/#:~:text=They%20founded%20the%20Global%20Impact,to%20invest%20in%20sustainable%20agriculture

7. Impact investing. The GIIN. (n.d.-b). https://thegiin.org/impact-investing

8. Omidyar Network's journey. Omidyar Network. (2022, October 21). https://omidyar.com/omidyar-networks-journey

9. Bannick, M., Goldman, P., Kubzansky, M., & Saltuk, Y. (n.d.). (rep.). Across The Returns Contiuum (pp. 1–22). Omidyar Network.

10. We invest in Early Care & Education through real estate. Mission Driven Finance™. (2024, March 20). https://www.missiondrivenfinance.com/invest/early-care-education/care-investment-trust

11. Omidyar Network supports DonorsChoose.org national expansion. Omidyar Network. (n.d.). https://medium.com/omidyar-network/why-we-invested-donorschoose-org-1e644cef0822

Chapter Two

1. The evolution of Heron. Heron Foundation. (2023, May 3). https://www.heron.org/enterprise

2. Foundation fact sheet (at a glance). Bill & Melinda Gates Foundation. (n.d.). https://www.gatesfoundation.org/about/foundation-fact-sheet

3. Piller, C., Sanders, E., & Dixon, R. (2007). Dark cloud over good works of Gates Foundation. Los Angeles Times. Retrieved 2024, from https://www.latimes.com/archives/la-xpm-2007-jan-07-na-gatesx07-story.html

4. Frequently asked questions: Strategic investment fund. Frequently Asked Questions | Strategic Investment Fund. (n.d.). https://sif.gates foundation.org/faq

5. Commissions + task forces. SIR RONALD COHEN. (n.d.). https:// sirronaldcohen.org/commissions-task-forces#:~:text=The%20Social %20Investment%20Task%20Force,social%20fabric%20in%20its%20 poorest

6. History: Our firm: Apax partners. Our Firm | Apax Partners. (n.d.). https://www.apax.com/our-firm/history

7. Cohen, R. (2020). *Impact: Reshaping Capitalism to Drive Real Change.* Ebury Press.

8. Our history. Big Society Capital. (n.d.). https://bigsocietycapital.com/ about-us/our-history

9. Investment into UK social impact exceeds £9 billion despite economic gloom. Big Society Capital. (n.d.-a). https://bigsocietycapital.com/ latest/investment-into-uk-social-impact-exceeds-9-billion-despite-economic-gloom

10. About. New Energy Nexus. (n.d.). https://www.newenergynexus.com/ about

11. Chapter 6: Divestment. Hampshire College. (n.d.). https://www.hampshire .edu/chapter-6-divestment

12. U.S. Mission to International Organization in Geneva. (2013). Pressure to End Apartheid Began at Grass Roots in U.S. https://geneva.usmission .gov/2013/12/17/pressure-to-end-apartheid-began-at-grass-roots-in-u-s

13. Knight, R. (n.d.). Sanctions, disinvestment, and U.S. corporations in South Africa. https://richardknight.homestead.com/files/uscor porations.htm

14. AMA Corporate Policies on Tobacco H-500.975. AMA. (n.d.). https:// policysearch.ama-assn.org/policyfinder/detail/tobacco?uri=%2FA MADoc%2FHOD.xml-0-4579.xml

Chapter Three

1. Global Sustainable Investment Alliance. (2023). (rep.). Global Sustainable Investment Review 2022. Retrieved 2024.

2. United Nations Global Compact. (2004). (rep.). Who Cares Wins. Retrieved 2024.

3. Home. IFRS. (n.d.). https://www.ifrs.org/about-us/who-we-are

4. Download SASB® Standards. SASB. (2024, January 29). https://sasb .ifrs.org/standards/download/?lang=en-us

5. (2020). J.B. Hunt Becomes First SASB Reporter in Road Transportation. Retrieved 2024, from https://sasb.ifrs.org/blog/jb-hunt-becomes-first-sasb-reporter-in-road-transportation

6. United Nations Environment Programme Finance Initiative. (2020). Our Partnership for Sustainable Capital Markets. Retrieved 2024, from https://www.gpif.go.jp/en/investment/Our_Partnership_for_Sustainable_ Capital_Markets.pdf

7. PRI. (2024, February 22). About the PRI. PRI. https://www.unpri.org/ about-us/about-the-pri

8. Principles for Responsible Investment. (2023). (rep.). 2022-23 Annual Report. Retrieved 2024, from https://dwtyzx6upklss.cloudfront.net/ Uploads/z/s/n/pri_ar2023_smaller_file_8875.pdf

Chapter Four

1. Our funds. Domini. (n.d.-b). https://domini.com/funds

Chapter Five

1. SJF ventures – high growth. positive impact.: Impact. SJF Ventures – High Growth. Positive Impact. | Impact. (n.d.). https://sjfventures .com/impact

2. Working to restoring the promise of Communities. About Us | Jonathan Rose. (n.d.). https://www.rosecompanies.com/about

3. Our firm – microvest – purposeful investing. MicroVest. (2023). https://microvestfund.com/our-firm

4. Our story. Bridges Fund Management. (n.d.). https://www.bridgesfund management.com/us/our-story

5. United Nations. (n.d.). The 17 goals | sustainable development. United Nations. https://sdgs.un.org/goals

6. United Nations. (n.d.-a). Goal 3 | Department of Economic and Social Affairs. United Nations. https://sdgs.un.org/goals/goal3#targets_and_indicators

7. Goel, S., & Kovacs-Ondrejkovic, O. (2023, January 26). Your strategy is only as good as your skills. BCG Global. https://www.bcg.com/publications/2023/your-strategy-is-only-as-good-as-your-skills

8. Brenan, M. (2023, January 17). Record high in U.S. put off medical care due to cost in 2022. Gallup.com. https://news.gallup.com/poll/468053/record-high-put-off-medical-care-due-cost-2022.aspx

9. https://www.worldbank.org/en/news/feature/2022/07/21/covid-19-boosted-the-adoption-of-digital-financial-services

Chapter Six

1. Domini Impact Equity Fund – Investor shares. Domini. (n.d.). https://domini.com/domini-funds/domini-impact-equity-fund

2. Community development finance. Self-Help Credit Union. (n.d.). https://www.self-help.org/what-we-do/we-learn-and-innovate/community-development-finance

3. Our story. Our Story | Amalgamated Bank. (n.d.). https://www.amalgamatedbank.com/our-story

4. Why first women's bank? About Us | First Women's Bank. (n.d.). https://www.firstwomens.bank/About-Us

5. Community investment note®. Calvert Impact. (n.d.). https://calvert impact.org/investing/community-investment-note

6. The evolution of Heron. Heron Foundation. (n.d.). https://www .heron.org/enterprise

7. Intentionally designed endowments. Intentional Endowments Network. (n.d.). https://www.intentionalendowments.org/about_ien

8. Final rule on Prudence and loyalty in selecting plan investments and exercising shareholder rights. U.S. Department of Labor. (n.d.). https://www.dol.gov/agencies/ebsa/about-ebsa/our-activities/resource-center/fact-sheets/final-rule-on-prudence-and-loyalty-in-selecting-plan-investments-and-exercising-shareholder-rights

Chapter Seven

1. Mission, vision, and values. ICIC. (n.d.). https://icic.org/about/mission-vision-and-values

2. The impact: About. The ImPact | About. (n.d.). https://www.the impact.org/about

3. Home. The Vistria Group. (n.d.-a). https://vistria.com

4. Reskilling revolution: Preparing 1 billion people for Tomorrow's economy. World Economic Forum. (n.d.). https://www.weforum.org/impact/reskilling-revolution-reaching-600-million-people-by-2030

Chapter Eight

1. Investment Company Act Rule 156 (1961).

2. Impact & Sustainable Finance Consortium. (n.d.). https://www.impact andsustainablefinance.org/index.html

3. About. Impact Capital Managers. (n.d.). https://www.impactcapital managers.com/about-us

Chapter Nine

1. Musk, Elon (@elonmusk). 2022. "Exxon is rated top ten best in world for environment, social & governance (ESG) by S&P 500, while Tesla didn't make the list! ESG is a scam. It has been weaponized by phony social justice warriors." X (formerly known as Twitter) May 18, 2022 11:09 AM. https://twitter.com/elonmusk/status/1526958110023245829

2. Wiggins, K., Evans, J., Massoudi, A., Gara, A., & Schipani, A. (2021, November 19). Bidders for unilever's tea business pulled out on plantation concerns. Financial Times. Retrieved 2024, from https://www.ft.com/content/5c7bbed1-c0ce-4767-a275-530b8ab9a1fc

3. Seventh Generation: More Than a Name. (January 1, 2022). Seventh Generation. https://www.seventhgeneration.com/blog/more-than-a-name

4. Out Impact. (n.d.). Seventh Generation. https://www.seventhgeneration.com/company/goals-impact

5. Lagorio-Chafkin, Christine. (July 18, 2009). "How Seventh Generation Became a Powerhouse Brand." Inc. Magazine. https://www.inc.com/christine-lagorio/seventh-generation-jeffrey-hollender-founders-project.html

6. Statista. (2023). (rep.). Natural household cleaners market value worldwide from 2019 to 2025 (in billion U.S. dollars). Retrieved 2024.

Chapter Ten

1. Trelstad, B. (2016). Making Sense of the Many Kinds of Impact Investing. *Harvard Business Review*.

2. About Luminaid. LuminAID. (n.d.). https://luminaid.com/pages/about-luminaid

Chapter Eleven

1. Syed, S. T., Gerber, B. S., & Sharp, L. K. (2013). Traveling towards disease: Transportation Barriers to Health Care Access. *Journal of Community Health*, 38(5), 976–993. https://doi.org/10.1007/s10900-013-9681-1
2. History of impact innovation & collaboration: Impact frontiers. Impact Frontiers icon frontiers small. (n.d.). https://impactfrontiers.org/history

Chapter Twelve

1. Tideline Publications with Impact Capital Managers. (2018). (rep.). The Alpha in Impact (pp. 1–42).
2. Tideline Publications with Impact Capital Managers. (2018). (rep.). The Alpha in Impact (pp. 1–42).
3. About B corps. B Lab U.S. & Canada. (n.d.). https://usca.bcorporation.net/about-b-corps
4. PBCs and the Pursuit of Public Good. Harvard Law School Forum on Corporate Governance. (2022). https://corpgov.law.harvard.edu/2022/12/09/pbcs-and-the-pursuit-of-corporate-good/#:~:text=Today%2C%20there%20are%2019%20publicly,operate%20these%20entities%20as%20subsidiaries

Chapter Thirteen

1. Investments – Lumos Capital Group: New York & San Francisco. Lumos Capital Group | New York & San Francisco. (n.d.). https://www.lumoscapitalgroup.com/investments
2. Why onlinemeded? Why OnlineMedEd? (n.d.). https://www.onlinemeded.com/why-ome

3. Diversity in medicine: Facts and figures 2019. AAMC. (n.d.). https://www.aamc.org/data-reports/workforce/report/diversity-medicine-facts-and-figures-2019

4. Building Better Lives. Edovo. (n.d.). https://www.edovo.com/justiced-impacted-learners

5. Impact correctional programming. Edovo. (n.d.-a). https://www.edovo.com

6. Impact correctional programming. Edovo. (n.d.-a). https://www.edovo.com

Chapter Fifteen

1. American Dream. (n.d.). Oxford English Dictionary. Retrieved 2024, from https://www.oed.com/search/dictionary/?scope=Entries&q=American+Dream

2. Poverty in the United States: 2022. (September 12, 2023). United States Census Bureau. https://www.census.gov/content/dam/Census/newsroom/press-kits/2023/iphi/20230912-iphi-slides-poverty.pdf

3. Federal Deposit Insurance Corporation. (2022). (rep.). 2021 FDIC National Survey of Unbanked and Underbanked Households – Executive Summary.

4. Annual Earnings By Educational Attainment. (May 2023). National Center for Education Statistics. https://nces.ed.gov/programs/coe/indicator/cba/annual-earnings

5. Coe – postsecondary outcomes for nontraditional and traditional undergraduate students. (n.d.). https://nces.ed.gov/programs/coe/indicator/ctu

6. Improving student literacy. BookNook. (n.d.). https://www.booknook.com/impact

7. America's Rental Housing 2024. (2024). Joint Center for Housing Studies of Harvard University. Harvard University Graduate School

of Design and Harvard Kennedy School. https://www.jchs.harvard
.edu/sites/default/files/reports/files/Harvard_JCHS_Americas_Rental_
Housing_2024.pdf

8. Expenses. The Fed – Expenses. (n.d.). https://www.federalreserve.gov/
publications/2023-economic-well-being-of-us-households-in-2022-
expenses.htm

Chapter Sixteen

1. Hartman, M., Martin, A. B., Whittle, L., & Catlin, A. (2024). National
Health Care Spending in 2022: Growth similar to prepandemic rates.
Health Affairs, 43(1), 6–17. https://doi.org/10.1377/hlthaff.2023.01360

2. https://www.oecd.org/health/health-at-a-glance

3. NVCA. (March 20, 2023). Value of venture capital (VC) investment in
the United States in 2022, by industry (in billion U.S. dollars) [Graph].
In Statista. Retrieved April 2, 2024, from https://www-statista-com
.proxy.uchicago.edu/statistics/423054/venture-capital-investments-usa-
by-industry

4. Private equity's role in Health Care. Commonwealth Fund. (2023,
November 17). https://www.commonwealthfund.org/publications/
explainer/2023/nov/private-equity-role-health-care

5. Reducing disparities in health care. American Medical Association.
(2023, October 23). https://www.ama-assn.org/delivering-care/patient-
support-advocacy/reducing-disparities-health-care

6. Steinberg, J. R. (2021, June 18). Female enrollment and
participantsexbyburdenofdiseaseinUSclinicaltrials.*JAMANetworkOpen.*
https://jamanetwork.com/journals/jamanetworkopen/fullarticle/
2781192?utm_source=PE2&utm_medium=email&utm_campaign=
07a024bf24-EMAIL_CAMPAIGN_2017_01_10_COPY_01&utm_
term=0_8f5769ea18-07a024bf24-

7. Langreth, R., & Campbell, M. (2022, April 19). Drug trials are more likely to admit white people. Bloomberg.com. https://www.bloomberg .com/news/articles/2022-04-19/drug-trials-are-more-likely-to-admit-white-people?utm_source=PE2&utm_campaign=07a024bf24-EMAIL_ CAMPAIGN_2017_01_10_COPY_01&utm_medium=email&utm_ term=0_8f5769ea18-07a024bf24-

8. Miller, L., & Tirrell, M. (2020, September 4). Moderna slows coronavirus vaccine trial enrollment to ensure minority representation, CEO says. CNBC. https://www.cnbc.com/2020/09/04/moderna-slows-coronavirus-vaccine-trial-t-to-ensure-minority-representation-ceo-says.html

9. Melek, S., Norris, D., Paulus, J., Matthews, K., Weaver, A., & Davenport, S. (n.d.). (rep.). Potential Economic Impact of Integrated Medical-Behavioral Healthcare (pp. 1–40). Milliman.

10. Mission. Workit Health. (n.d.). https://www.workithealth.com/mission

11. Eliason, N. (2020, August 7). Oatly: The new coke. Every. https://every .to/almanack/oatly-the-new-coke-821556

12. Oatly. (n.d.). (rep.). The Oatly Sustainability Report Update 2022 (pp. 1–57).

Chapter Seventeen

1. PWC. (n.d.). State of Climate Tech 2023: Investment analysis. State of Climate Tech 2023. https://www.pwc.com/gx/en/issues/esg/state-of-climate-tech-2023-investment.html

2. Tang, D. (2023, February). Climate tech's evolution: The maturation to a competitive, returns-focused thematic investment sector. Cambridge Associates. https://www.cambridgeassociates.com/insight/climate-techs-evolution

3. Renewable power generation costs in 2022. IRENA. (2023, August 1). https://www.irena.org/Publications/2023/Aug/Renewable-Power-Generation-Costs-in-2022

4. PWC. (n.d.). State of Climate Tech 2023: Investment analysis. State of Climate Tech 2023. https://www.pwc.com/gx/en/issues/esg/state-of-climate-tech-2023-investment.html

5. Perfect power – about Us. (n.d.). https://www.perfectpowerllc.com/about/sum.html

6. Watkins, F. (2017, August 8). A shocking 80 percent of Americans can't access rooftop solar. Here's why. Solstice. https://solstice.us/solstice-blog/why-americans-cant-access-rooftop-solar

7. About. Twelve. (n.d.). https://www.twelve.co/about

8. World Bank Group. (2018, September 20). Global waste to grow by 70 percent by 2050 unless urgent action is taken: World Bank Report. World Bank. https://www.worldbank.org/en/news/press-release/2018/09/20/global-waste-to-grow-by-70-percent-by-2050-unless-urgent-action-is-taken-world-bank-report

9. Towards zero waste accelerator. C40 Cities. (n.d.). https://www.c40.org/accelerators/zero-waste

10. McKinsey & Company. (2021, November 8). Protecting people from a changing climate: The case for resilience. McKinsey & Company. https://www.mckinsey.com/capabilities/sustainability/our-insights/protecting-people-from-a-changing-climate-the-case-for-resilience

11. Our story. Gotham Greens. (n.d.). https://www.gothamgreens.com/our-story

12. Global fossil fuel divestment database. Global Fossil Fuel Commitments Database. (n.d.). https://divestmentdatabase.org

Chapter Eighteen

1. 2023 proxy season review. (n.d.). https://www.conference-board.org/press/2023-proxy-season-review

2. European Investment Bank. (n.d.). Climate awareness bonds. (CAB). https://www.eib.org/en/OLD-investor_relations/cab/index .htm#:~:text=In%202007%2C%20the%20EIB%20issued,of%20 6.8bn%20in%202020

3. Green bonds. World Bank. (n.d.). https://treasury.worldbank.org/en/ about/unit/treasury/ibrdibrd-green-bonds#:~:text=In%202008%2C%20 the%20World%20Bank,to%20encourage%20within%20this%20 framework

4. Single-Family Green MBS. Single-Family Green MBS | Fannie Mae. (n.d.). https://capitalmarkets.fanniemae.com/sustainable-bonds/green-bonds/single-family-green-mbs

5. Green bond. PepsicoUpgrade. (n.d.). https://www.pepsico.com/our-impact/esg-topics-a-z/green-bond

6. Gardiner, J. (2024, February 8). Green bonds reached new heights in 2023 | insights | bloomberg professional services. Bloomberg.com. https://www.bloomberg.com/professional/insights/trading/green-bonds-reached-new-heights-in-2023

Chapter Nineteen

1. Impact bonds. Social Finance. (n.d.). https://www.socialfinance.org .uk/what-we-do/social-impact-bonds#:~:text=Social%20Finance%20 set%20up%20the,key%20part%20of%20our%20approach

2. Impact bond dataset. The Government Outcomes Lab. (n.d.). https:// golab.bsg.ox.ac.uk/knowledge-bank/indigo/impact-bond-dataset-v2

Chapter Twenty

1. https://www.weforum.org/agenda/2015/07/how-does-income-inequality-affect-economic-growth/

2. What is an ESOP and how does it work?. What Is an ESOP (Employee Stock Ownership Plan)? | ESOP.org. (n.d.). https://www

.esop.org/#:~:text=ESOP%20Map%20of%20the%20U.S.,over%20
%242.1%20trillion%20in%20assets

3. Employee Ownership Foundation. (n.d.). ESOPs and retirement wealth inequality. ESOPs and Retirement Wealth Inequality | Employee Ownership Foundation. https://www.employeeownershipfoundation .org/articles/esops-and-retirement-wealth-inequality

4. What is an ESOP and how does it work? What Is an ESOP (Employee Stock Ownership Plan)? | ESOP.org. (n.d.). https://www .esop.org/#:~:text=ESOP%20Map%20of%20the%20U.S.,over%20 %242.1%20trillion%20in%20assets

5. Blasi, J., Kruse, D., & Weltmann, D. (2013). (rep.). "Firm Survival and Performance in Privately-Held ESOP Companies," Sharing Ownership, Profits, and Decision-Making in the 21st Century (Vol. 14, pp. 109– 124). Advances in the Economic Analysis of Participatory & Labor-Managed Firms.

6. The Story – Firebrand Artisan Breads – Oakland's Only Wood-Fired Bakery. (n.d.). https://www.firebrandbread.com/the-story

7. Purpose Economy. (n.d.). (rep.). Firebrand Artisan Breads – Case Study.

8. Yvon Chouinard donates Patagonia to fight climate crisis. Patagonia Outdoor Clothing & Gear. (n.d.). https://www.patagonia.com/ownership

Conclusion

1. The Rise Fund. (n.d.). https://therisefund.com

Acknowledgments

THE CONTENTS OF THIS book came from the guidance and encouragement I've received from colleagues, mentors, clients, investees, family, and friends over the past two decades. The lessons that I've shared came from both successes and failures. Attempting to list all the people who shaped me over the years would inevitably be incomplete. However, I'd like to acknowledge those who directly supported the book from conception to completion.

Bill Falloon at John Wiley & Sons deserves credit for the vision and persistence that impact investing be part of the Little Book series. Thank you, Bill, for giving me the honor of writing this book.

Special thanks to David Press and Imogen Rose-Smith at Confluence Partners, who convinced me to take this opportunity and who worked as editors to ensure that the book's structure and stories supported the content I wanted to share with the world. I could not have done this without you.

My partners at Impact Engine might as well be coauthors as so much of what I know comes from our work together. Jessica Droste Yagan, Roger Liew, and Tasha Seitz, I hope you can see that I've been taking notes on all your wisdom. I am proud of what we are building, and even prouder of how we're building it.

Robert Gertner, Caroline Grossman, and Christina Hachikian gave me the opportunity to begin teaching impact investing at Chicago Booth, which was the catalyst for much of the content in this book. Thank you for your continued support of my work and the impact investing field.

I was fortunate to have several trusted friends read early versions of the book and provide valuable feedback. You each brought a unique lens to your suggestions, complementing my own views and skills to make the book even stronger. Thank you to Rahul Bhide, Diana Callaghan, Jessica Droste Yagan, Sophia Friedman, Dan Harris, John Hoeppner, Ander Irureta-goyena, Young Kwak, Roger Liew, Chuck Parrish, Kim Vender Moffat, and Chris Wu.

Rebecca, you are the instigator of this story. I am forever grateful for that bus ride and your questions that made me believe this was all possible. Thank you for pushing me to be an impact investor long before it became my job.

Mom and Dad, I owe everything to you. Your sacrifice, inspiration, and support for me are the backbone to my life. Thousands look up to you from afar, but I am honored to get the up-close experience. Thank you for always seeing the best in me so that I could see it in myself.

Sai, Aadi, and Diya, I love you with all my heart. Thank you for being patient beyond your years as I wrote this book. You make me so proud and are the greatest impact of my life.

About the Author

───────────── ∾ ─────────────

Pʀɪʏᴀ Pᴀʀʀɪsʜ ɪs ᴀ partner and chief investment officer at Impact Engine, an institutional venture capital and private equity investor driving positive impact in economic opportunity, environmental sustainability, and health equity. She is also an adjunct assistant professor of strategy and the impact investor in residence at the University of Chicago Booth School of Business and serves as an adviser to investment firms developing and managing impact investment strategies. Prior to joining Impact Engine, Priya served as chief investment officer at Schwartz Capital Group, a single-family office investing across global markets. Previously, she was the strategy head at Aurora Investment Management, a multibillion-dollar hedge fund, and managed the development of investment products that incorporated environmental, social, and governance (ESG) factors at Northern Trust Asset Management and KLD Research & Analytics. Crain's Chicago Business named her to its list of 40-Under-40 and Notable LGBTQ Executives. Priya has a BS in business management from Babson College and an MBA from the University of Chicago Booth School of Business.